Love Abides: The Sacrament of Grieving

By Sue Magrath

LOVE ABIDES

The Sacrament of Grieving

Other Books by Sue Magrath

Healing the Ravaged Soul: Tending the Spiritual Wounds of Child Sexual Abuse
My Burden is Light: A Primer for Clergy Wellness
The Salvation of Poetry: A Novel

For Juli, who was the impetus for this book but didn't live to see it completed.

Table of Contents

Introduction

I must admit that in the beginning of the pandemic, it felt like a prolonged "snow day." Everything got cancelled—meetings, speaking engagements, church. For the first time in a while, I had the space in which to finish the novel I had been working on for five years. Sure, I missed seeing my neighbors and friends, my kids and grandkids, but the words were pouring out of me and onto the page in a torrent, and I was loving it.

But then reality began to set in. I grieved for the tens of thousands who were dying across the country and around the world. I shed tears over the crowded COVID wards on my TV screen and the bodies in body bags piled high in trucks to be taken to overrun mortuaries. I grieved for the medical personnel who were terrified by the shortage of PPE's and overwhelmed by all the COVID patients dying alone in ICU without the comfort of loved ones.

Then the personal losses began to pile up. My son lost his job. My daughter's marriage collapsed. Both my mother-in-law and father-in-law were diagnosed with cancer. After a few months of treatment, my mother-in-law died, and her death bed became a super-spreader event. My father-in-law had been coughing, but nobody thought anything of it. He was scheduled for surgery to remove his cancerous kidney two days after his wife passed away, and after helping make funeral arrangements, my husband dropped him off at the hospital on his way back home. When he started coughing too, he went to get tested and was determined to be positive for the coronavirus. He called the hospital to let them know they'd better test his father, and sure enough, he also had COVID. His case was quite severe, and he almost lost his life.

Somewhere along the line in this chain of events, our son announced that he and his wife were expecting baby number two. It was great to have something to be happy about until the doctors discovered that the baby might have a rare genetic disorder. Our daughter-in-law had an amniocentesis to confirm the diagnosis, and after a torturous ten-day wait, we found out that the baby did not have the disorder after all.

This news came when I was enjoying a much-needed getaway with three of my closest friends with whom I shared a deep spiritual bond. I had told them about the possibility of my grandson being born with a deadly genetic disorder, and we had all shed tears over the woes of the world, both personal and global. We agreed that it was just too much. And when I got the news that my grandson would be fine, they also shared my joy.

It was during that weekend, in the context of telling my story, listening to the stories of my friends, and realizing how much weight I had been carrying that I realized I needed to write a book about grief. And I knew that this book needed to be one that looked at loss, not just from a psychological standpoint, but a spiritual one as well, exploring the ways that faith is changed by grief, and how grief is impacted by faith. I wanted it to be a book of stories. Real people, real grief—not the grief you read about from articles about stages and how-to's, but real stories that defy categories and give readers permission to grieve however they need to rather than what they've internalized from their families, the media, psychologists, and the advice of friends.

And so began this journey. I spent a full year interviewing people who had suffered loss, listening to their stories, and asking them how they got through the most painful experiences of their lives. I was deeply touched by their stories and by their trust in me to hear them and share them in ways that honored their lost loved ones. I was moved by their honesty and vulnerability. And I came to understand this one thing—that ultimately, this would be a book about love. We do not grieve what we have not loved. People may die, but our love for them does not. That's why it hurts so much. Love abides, even when it hurts.

This book is not meant to be read straight through. Take your time with it. Linger over the parts that invite you to process, pray, or ponder. Take time to engage in the spiritual practices at the end of each chapter. Pray the prayers and let them sink deep into your soul. There are interludes after the prayer that draw you deeper into a time of contemplation, that ask you to pause before moving on to the next chapter. You may find it helpful to record your thoughts, feelings, and insights as you travel the byways of your journey of grief with the aid of this book. Blessings to you on this journey.

"And now faith, hope, and love abide, these three; and the greatest of these is love." —I Corinthians 13:13 (NRSV)

Chapter One

Our Common Humanity

"Grieving is not an orderly process. Grief is the least linear thing I know. . .. Grief tends to be unruly. . .. unpredictable and wild." Jan Richardson[1]

One of the universal experiences of life is that we will lose people we love. We cannot escape loss or the heartache of grief—nor should we want to. Though painful, grief is also holy. It is the final act of devotion to the ones we have loved and lost. Through our grief, we honor them, our tears an anointing and sacred act. Nonetheless, it is an experience that sets us apart from the everyday world where other people go about their business as if tragedy had never touched them. As an old Vogues song goes, "Why does the sun go on shining, why does the sea rush to shore, don't they know it's the end of the world . . .?"[2] When we are drowning in grief, we wonder how or whether we can ever re-enter the land of the living.

Many writers, psychologists, and spiritual leaders have attempted to provide a road map for the journey of

---

[1] Richardson, *The Cure for Sorrow: A Book of Blessings for Times of Grief, 13.*

[2] Skeeter Davis, *The End of the World,* 1962

grief, some helpful and some not, but there still remains a hunger for guidance and comfort during these difficult times. We keep looking for a magic formula that will help us navigate this strange territory in which we find ourselves, so that we can get back to "normal" as soon as possible. But normal is elusive, and the pain is not eased by knowing the stages of grief or how many of them we have to go through before we don't hurt so much anymore.

As the opening quote states, grief is unpredictable and wild, often failing to cooperate with our desire to corral it or bring it under our control. Tears fall when they feel like it, no matter where you are or with whom. You are assailed with conflicting emotions at every turn, experiencing rage, guilt, fear, despair, longing, or emptiness, sometimes all in the same day or same hour. And that's okay. There is no one way to grieve. Grief refuses to be confined to any theory, model, or formula for the journey from heartache to healing. There is no right way to grieve. The only thing you can do is submit to it, feel what you feel, and know that it can change on a dime.

Many of us would like to avoid grief altogether, long to run away from it, pretend we are fine. Not only is this impossible, but even the attempt diminishes our humanity and denies us the comfort we might receive from family, friends, and the stranger sitting next to us on the bus.

> In this biological world we can see clearly that death is a stage in the life cycle. In our human case, we cling to the precious consciousness that seems to set us apart

from the rest of the natural world, and we see death with different eyes—as an ending, often cruel, and sometimes unendurable.

We do ourselves no service to make an enemy of death; it is a presence within our life, and by denying it, we deny a part of ourselves. Our deepest knowledge includes a knowledge of death. To experience loss and to grieve are (two of) the great common human experiences, and to deny them is to make ourselves less human.

We live in a beautifully balanced system in which death is a part of everything that lives. The pain of our personal loss is ours; within the greater whole, nothing is lost. Perhaps it is too much to say that we will ever understand death; the fruit of time and pain and healing is that we will come to accept it.[3]

Perhaps a journal entry I wrote following my mother's death will help to illustrate this point about our shared humanity:

I awoke that dreary fall day, my mood a reflection of the weather. It was the day of my mother's memorial service. Despite years of watching her descent into soul-stealing dementia, I found that I was no more prepared for Mom's death than if she

---

[3] "The Promise of a New Day," Hazeldon Meditation Series, 1983 (July 27 reading)

had died from a sudden heart attack. I had grieved plenty during those years, grieved the loss of her essence and her mothering, but none of that lessened how slammed I felt now by the loss of her life and breath.

The next few days brought the hard work of packing up Mom's things. I found myself derailed by finding her old library card or a hand-written grocery list. My husband and adult children had their own meltdowns over a photograph or journal entry, but my grandson's two-year-old antics helped us smile and move on. Somewhere underneath the activity and overwhelming emotion, I realized how precious it all was.

The following week, I was back in my counseling office, praying for strength and objectivity through the workday ahead. My first client burst into tears the minute she saw me. A close friend had died suddenly, and my client's sorrow was palpable. Inwardly, I thought, "You've got to be kidding me, God!" I didn't know how I was going to keep it together, and in fact, I didn't. Instead of offering calm reassurance, I cried with her as she processed her grief. We shared stories of our loved ones, and I felt that our tears were like precious oil anointing our cheeks and honoring the dead.

Early in the afternoon, a young woman whose aunt was battling cancer arrived. She immediately announced that the doctors had given her aunt days to live. I felt a weight settle in my chest. Not again! Again, I sent up a wordless plea for strength and guidance. Again, tears came, sorrowing for this girl who was losing the woman who loved her more than her own mother.

My final client of the day told me her grandfather was in hospice. I couldn't help thinking that God had a sick sense of humor, yet as the session went on, I began to see the blessing in it all. My tears gave all these women permission to cry. My grief showed them it is acceptable to feel pain even if we know our loved one's death is a blessed release. Sharing my own grief helped them know they were not alone. And neither was I. At the end of the day, though exhausted and emptied, I understood that I had received the greater gift, that in the transforming power of shared loss, I had begun to heal.

"Grief is our common bond. Opening to sorrow connects us with everyone, everywhere." — Francis Weller[4]

---

[4] Weller, *The Wild Edge of Sorrow*

Sharon's Story

Sharon's father was a social worker and the kind of guy every kid wants for a dad—kind, playful, and loving. He had a great laugh. He wrote poetry. All this in spite of a stroke he suffered in midlife that resulted in disabilities that required regular care from his wife. In later years, he was diagnosed with prostate cancer. Two years into his treatment, he became extremely ill and was forced to abandon that treatment, which led to the unchecked growth of his cancer. Despite the pain, this man was determined to have a "good death." In his final year of life, he spoke openly with his family about what was happening to him, sometimes with tears as he contemplated the end of his life. He let them know what he wanted for his memorial service and chose favorite pictures of himself posing with loved ones to be shared during the service. He wrote poetry about his journey toward eternity, looked forward to being welcomed by the communion of saints, and reminisced about happy memories with his family.

One of the things that gave him peace in his final days was listening to a recording of bird song. At the moment of his death, with family by his side, a flock of geese flew by his hospital window, honking as they went. It felt as though the Holy Spirit had come to carry his soul to heaven.

Sharon describes her father's death as both hard and beautiful. "It was holy ground," she said, both life-giving and sacred. Though she was unhappy with his body for all the suffering it had caused, she was nonetheless grateful that it been the tangible vessel by which she and her family were able to experience his heart and soul in their lives. Despite the blessings that had manifested in her father's final days, the thing she experienced most in the immediate aftermath was deep fatigue. There was so much to do, so many people wanting to express their condolences, when all she wanted to do was be alone and cry. And she did—for months. Shortly after her father's death, she watched a documentary about Fred Rogers. She was an emotional mess through the whole program, because her father had loved Mr. Rogers, and Sharon saw so much of her father in him—his gentle manner and his total acceptance of others.

One of the hardest things for Sharon to do in her grief was to return to her parents' home. She couldn't imagine walking into that space full of memories and not find him there. It took a long time before she could bring herself to confront his absence from their house. She found comfort in reading his poetry. She still experiences his presence as a guiding force when she's unsure about how to handle difficult situations. She asks herself, "I wonder what my dad would have done, how he would embody grace in this moment?" She goes to places she had been with him, particularly a special tree where they would often sit and talk. If you asked her, Sharon would say that her father is still with her every day, but sometimes the tears still come. And she knows that's okay.

Grief Fallacies

There are many fallacies around death and grief that are part of our cultural belief system and can become stumbling blocks on our journey of grief. We get messages from many different sources that might trip us up if we believe everything we've been told about how grief unfolds.

- *Grief follows a predictable pattern of shock, anger, bargaining, depression, and acceptance.* These stages were hypothesized by Elizabeth Kubler-Ross based on her work with terminally ill patients in the late 1960's. It was not based on controlled psychological methods but on her observations and relationships with people who were approaching death, and in this particular context, it makes sense. As a predictor for the grief process, it might not fit for you. Someone who is grieving might go through all of these aspects of loss in a single day, maybe even more than once. Also, the stage of bargaining seems irrelevant to a loss that has already occurred. Bargaining is about making deals with God in hopes that God will save us from dire circumstances. In the case of the terminally ill, someone is pledging to become a better person if God will only save them from their fate. But when someone is dead, that ship has sailed. There are only two people that God ever brought back from the dead—Lazarus and Jesus—so bargaining is not a logical stage in the grieving process. In short, your grief is going to unfold in its own way without reference to any kind of grief model that exists in the psychological literature.

- *Anticipatory grief.* This concept suggests that knowing your loved one is nearing death due to illness or old age allows you to begin grieving before they are gone, and this will make the grief you experience at their death somewhat less intense and painful. While this in-between time does give you an opportunity to brace yourself for what is to come and achieve some level of acceptance, it doesn't change the blow you feel when your loved one is no longer breathing air on this earth. You will still have grieving to do. A pastor friend, Joan, lost her wife to brain cancer after a year of watching her suffer, observing the gradual loss of faculties, speech, and ability to function. She told me, "I thought I was ready (for her to go)," but the reality of her death was still excruciatingly painful. "I wanted to be where she was." While the worst of this level of pain eventually passed, it is still a daily ache for her.
- *It will take about a year to get over your grief.* Certainly, the first year is often the hardest as you experience the first birthdays, holidays, and anniversaries with all their attendant traditions without your loved one, but grief does not have an expiration date. It may subside over time, allow you to get accustomed to that person being gone, but you never get over your grief. You just learn to live with it. The painful memories will eventually come less often, but they can still surprise you when you

least expect it, bringing with them the intensity of a fresh loss. And for some, loss comes with so many logistical tasks—removing a spouse's or parent's name from accounts, dealing with insurance companies and Social Security, planning memorials, responding to donations, gifts, flowers, etc.—that grief can get shoved into the background until these practical matters are done. This can prolong the deepest period of grief. One woman I interviewed spent so much of the first year after her husband's death dealing with details of his considerable estate and business dealings that it wasn't until the second year that she was blindsided by the raw emotion of grief that flooded her. It was only then, when her now empty days allowed time for the pain to burst into her consciousness, that she felt the full brutal blow of loss.

The following poem illustrates how grief refuses to conform to a timeline, instead lingering long after the initial grieving is past:

> Nine years ago, my mom
> transcended the confines
> of her body
> to achieve ultimate healing
> in the arms of the Divine.
> I still miss her,
> sometimes fiercely,
> achingly.
> She loves me
> from a different dimension now,

love transmitted,
not through her gaze,
her words, her embrace,
but through memory
and a sense of her presence
when I am transported
by beauty.
But sometimes
I still feel her hand
lying gentle on my cheek.

Impediments to Grief

Ultimately, grief is a healing process, one that can lead to negative consequences if ignored, avoided, and/or suppressed. Some of these consequences are depression, the blunting of emotion, psychosomatic symptoms, and loss of connection with others. We resist or ignore grief at our peril. The following story is an allegory for what can happen when we ignore any kind of wound, whether physical or emotional.

When my son was small, he came to me one day and showed me his hand, asking, "What is this?" I could see a small white spot on his palm, but it didn't seem to be painful, so without any hint of injury, I told him that we would just keep an eye on it. Within a couple of days, the white spot was larger and looked like a small pocket of puss. I took him to the doctor, and he said it was likely an infection caused by a small sliver that had gone undetected. He then gently evacuated the puss and removed the offending sliver from my son's hand. He told me that if I had ignored the wound much longer, the infection could have gotten much worse and required deeper excision, causing my son more pain and requiring antibiotics to treat it. I have told this story to clients for years to illustrate the dangers of "burying" painful life events, including their grief.

Grief will have its way. It bides its time. It might sit in the background for a while, but ultimately it will find ways of expression that you don't have any control over. It can erupt when you are least expecting it and at a time when you are in a situation that requires a calm and steady demeanor. During my daughter's senior year of high school, my mother was diagnosed with dementia, and my pastor, a man I had often turned to for support and comfort, was being re-appointed to a different church. These three losses conspired to put me on shaky ground. I became very emotional and found myself crying over every sad song that came on the radio in my car. Knowing that it wouldn't be appropriate to burst into random tears in the midst of a counseling session, I decided I needed to address my grief more deliberately. I set aside a time when I had nothing else scheduled, shut myself in my bedroom, and let the grief out of its cage. I cried for over an hour. I spilled out my feelings about my daughter moving away to college, the loss of my mother's mental capacity, and the loss of the pastor who would normally have been the person who would walk with me through it all. And it helped. Afterwards, I felt a sense of calm. Even though I knew that these impending events would still be difficult and painful, I felt that I would be able to handle them without completely falling apart. By acknowledging and expressing my grief, I was able to breathe again.

"Grief is not a disorder, a disease, or a sign of weakness. It is an emotional, physical, and spiritual necessity, the price you pay for love. The only cure for grief is to grieve."[5]

But what makes some people feel the need to bury their grief deep inside and never let it see the light of day? For some, the answer might be found in the messages they received from their families about grief and tears. A close friend of mine lost a beloved grandfather when she was ten years old. At the graveside service, she burst into tears, grieving this man who had been so special to her, a source of affection and unconditional love. Seeing her weeping, her father came over to her, grabbed her by the arm, and pulled her away from the gathered crowd. "You stop crying right this minute! I never want to see you crying about this again!" From that moment, this woman learned that tears were unacceptable. As an adult, she tried hard not to allow painful emotions, but was often unsuccessful. When those times came that she could not control the tears, she would immediately call herself a "crybaby" and apologize for her inability to "buck up."

My father was also averse to tears, but the message was less overt, and my affectionate and empathetic mother counteracted that mindset. Nonetheless, I was somewhat amused when I called to see how my mother was handling

[5] Grollman, mygriefassist.com

the death of a good friend. The funeral had just been held earlier in the day. My father was the one to answer the phone, so I asked him how he and mom were doing. His response was, "Oh, fine. It was a good service. Nobody cried." I nearly laughed at his characterization of a good funeral as one in which nobody shed a tear! But, since the woman who died was also my sister's mother-in-law, I am quite sure that my sister wept a stream of tears. My dad's aversion to crying was particularly notable when my mother was descending deeper into dementia and living in a memory care facility. He and I had an unspoken agreement: When I came to visit her, I could cry if I had to, but if I did, he would walk right past me and ignore the tears completely.

A former client had lost her baby sister when she was five years old and her sister was just a toddler. Her first vivid memory is of paramedics racing into the house in the middle of the night to rush her sister to the hospital. After she died, the house became a shrine of photos and memorabilia, yet her sister was rarely mentioned in conversation, much less reminisced about. Many others have families in which a dead sibling or parent is never spoken of after their untimely death.

These kinds of experiences often lead to difficulty in expressing grief. People who receive these messages often end up suppressing not only grief, but *any* negative emotion. The problem is that when you suppress one emotion, you often suppress them all. The full spectrum of human emotion is no longer available to you, and your zest for life is diminished.

Another impediment to fully addressing grief is our societal messages about keeping a stiff upper lip and just getting on with life. Grief makes other people uncomfortable. They fear that your pain might open up the deep well of their own. And so, they offer platitudes, a pat on the shoulder, and an admonition that the dead person would want them to move on with their lives, so buck up. (See more about this in Chapter Nine). Not only is getting over it virtually impossible, but it is also not healthy. Your grief honors the dead. It is a measure of how much they were loved. What the people who try to shut down your grief fail to understand is that "...sorrow carves riverbeds in our soul, deepening us as it flows in and out of our lives."[6] That depth makes us richer and more compassionate human beings.

Other Types of Loss

We make a mistake when we limit the parameters of grief to the death of a loved one. There are many losses that do not involve an actual death but can be just as painful. Our communal experience of the COVID pandemic was a massive grief event, not only due to the overwhelming numbers of deaths, but from the loss of normal life experiences that we often take for granted, like gathering with family, friends, and neighbors, traveling, worshipping together in our churches, eating in a restaurant. We learned that ZOOM and Facetime were

[6] Weller, *The Wild Edge of Sorrow,* p. 1

blessings that allowed us to conduct business and stay connected to one another, but nothing replaces a good hug. The loss of regular human touch impacted everyone, no matter what their circumstances.

A former pastor of mine once said, "We experience little deaths every day." Some of these other deaths include divorce, job loss, estrangement from family members, and the loss of a true childhood due to abuse, trauma, and/or neglect. Any significant changes in our lives, even positive ones, can have an aspect of grief. Most of these "little deaths" contain some element of the Dream—the dream of a perfect marriage, an important career, a loving family, a happy life. When those things don't happen or there is a bump in the road that changes what once was good into a loss of our hopes and dreams, we suffer. Divorce is especially difficult, even when there's no joy left in the marriage, or it was a conflictual or abusive relationship. When we marry, it becomes part of our identity. When the relationship ends, that piece of who we were is gone. Being a wife or husband is no longer who we are. We live in a coupled society, and social events are often centered around couples. When you are no longer part of a couple, you can feel invisible and left out.

Another aspect of losing a spouse to death or divorce is the loss of a helpmate, someone who is a partner in all of the tasks and responsibilities of being a family—paying the bills, cooking, cleaning, yardwork, taking the kids to school, helping them with homework, etc. And one of the often unspoken losses is the loss of a sexual partner. This is not something we feel comfortable sharing with others, but it is just as significant as some of the other factors in this type of loss. Physical touch is essential to a sense of well-being, and sexual intimacy is a major part of that. It's important to consciously grieve the loss of intimacy and find ways to fill that need, whether through hugs from friends, getting an affectionate and cuddly pet, or getting a massage.

Speaking of pets, losing a beloved pet is often just as hard as losing a person with whom you have a close relationship—some might say harder. They give us unconditional love that we can always count on even when the humans around us don't. Pets are an integral part of our everyday lives, a member of the family, a loving companion, and at times a comforting presence when troubles arise. When they are gone, there are so many reminders that bring tears. Our first dog, Skeeter, loved to lay at our feet. Whether we were sitting on the sofa or in an easy chair, he had to be right there underfoot. We had become so accustomed to watching where we stepped every time we got up from our seat that we continually expected him to be there long after he was gone. And every time was an occasion for tears. Another of our dogs, Maggie, who died during the pandemic, habitually met us at the door whenever we came home from an outing, jumping up to greet us and letting us know that we had been gone too long, whether it was a quick errand or an evening out. It took a long time for us to stop expecting her to be there whenever we pulled into the garage.

Unfortunately, the grief we feel over our pet's loss is sometimes minimized by others. Someone who has never had a pet just cannot understand the depth of our grief. "It's just an animal," they might say. They don't realize the deep connections we have, the memories that our animals are connected to. Another of our dogs had belonged to my parents, but when my mom had to be placed in a memory care facility for her dementia, my dad didn't think he could adequately care for little Peekaboo any longer. I brought her home with me, and she became ours. Years later, when we had to put her to sleep, it was a loss not only of her, but of that connection to both my parents, who had since passed away.

I believe it is so important to acknowledge the depth of our grief over lost pets. Let yourself mourn; let the tears fall. Don't pay attention to those people who would minimize your loss. Grief over our four-legged friends is real and lasting. You may want to find some ritual to celebrate their life—burying their ashes at the base of a favorite tree, donating their toys to an animal shelter, or creating a scrapbook of photos with them.

Our careers are another part of our Dream, so when something happens to disrupt or deny the job of our dreams, it is a major loss. I had always wanted to be a teacher and a writer. I lasted in the teaching profession for a year and a half before quitting due to a difficult principal. There was a glut of teachers on the job market at the time, and I was unable to find another teaching job. I grieved that loss and struggled for years to discern my vocational identity. I did eventually, but the in-between time was fraught with frustration and disappointment. Often, we aren't given to know the happy end of the story, and it's only later that we see the ways God was working in our lives. I came to understand that as a therapist, I was also an educator, and my work ultimately led me to write four books.

Children often dream of becoming a professional sports figure, a model, a firefighter, or police officer, but sometimes those goals are unrealistic or out of reach. When those dreams don't pan out, some people feel a loss of identity for the rest of their lives. Grieving the loss of this dream means accepting the circumstances and exploring other ways to live a significant life, even if we never achieve fame and fortune.

Unlike in earlier times, the modern world has become a much more mobile society. For centuries, most people stayed in the same town or city for generations, while the people of today are more likely to move several times in their lifetime. This means that we lose our connection to place whenever we pick up stakes and move on for a better job, a bigger house, a change of climate or scenery. If we put down roots in each of these places, the act of pulling them up again is a loss in itself. I was raised on a lake resort in northeastern Washington state, where we lived for the first eleven years of my life. The spirit of this place lives in my bones. A few years ago, my husband and I took our trailer there for a vacation. As evening fell, I walked down to the swimming dock, dangled my feet in the water, and wept. I felt a deep connection to the physicality of this lake, the sky and stars above, the surrounding hillsides forming a bowl in the earth. The sense of place, of belonging to this unique land and water, held me in its embrace. My gratitude for the land that had birthed me overwhelmed me. And I grieved what I had lost so many years ago. Since my childhood, there have been many more losses of place—from the Pacific Ocean to the stark beauty of Alaska to the deserts of Arizona, to a small town in the middle of Washington. Every time we moved, I could feel the tearing loose of moorings that had held me in place—friends, self-discovery, vocation, the stages of our children's growth, and the unique experiences of the land itself. And each time, I grieved. In each place, I had been woven into the fabric of a community, and unraveling those connections was painful. But the sadness of leaving was tempered by gratitude for the ways in which the land and the people had shaped and blessed me.

Another deep loss is family estrangement—adult siblings who cut other family members out of their lives, adult children whose animosity toward their parents leads them to withhold contact from grandchildren, parents who disown their young adult offspring for making choices they disagree with. These losses are extraordinarily painful. I worked with many clients who experienced this kind of deep loss and struggled to help them make sense of it. In the end, all I could do was offer comfort, validation and a safe place to process their grief.

One of the most painful losses this side of death is the loss of a happy and healthy childhood. Victims of trauma, whether through physical, sexual, or emotional abuse, suffer greatly from their loss of a "normal" childhood. They will never know what it is like to have parents who loved and protected them, whose physical touch was affectionate and comforting rather than painful, frightening, and/or a corruption of their flesh. For these victims, healing takes time, a good therapist, and supportive allies to help them process the grief that never ends.

As you can see, grief is not limited to death, but is a part of every loss we experience in life. Grief is one of the many things that unites us, that helps us see how important love is, how sacred. Grief is a sacrament in which we offer ourselves and our loved ones up to God, receiving comfort and love in return.

Spiritual Practice

Let your mind wander through some of the losses you have experienced in your life and the way that your grief manifested itself in you. Take time to remember the people you've lost, how much you loved them, the ways in which they impacted your life both when they were alive as well as the ways they still live on in your heart and mind. How do you continue to honor them with the way that you live your life? Offer up a prayer of thanks for the gift of memories and the people, places and things that still bind them to you.

Prayer

Holy One, we give you thanks for the gift of the loved ones who have left us for existence on another plane. Help us to remember and cherish the love they gave us and the love we carry in our hearts because they were in our lives. Help us know that grief is the natural aftermath of loss, and that expressing grief does not follow a formula but flows from the fountain of our love, both given and received. We know that human love is but a whisper of your love for us, and we give you thanks. Amen.

Interlude

One Would Think
One would think
one would become accustomed
to grief,
year after year
as the losses,
both large and small,
begin to pile up.
One would think
we'd get better at it.
But no.
Loss can still
knock our legs
out from under us,
turn our careful plans
into rubble,
turn our carefully constructed life
into a debris field.
What can we do
but pick up the pieces
one by one,
salvage the blessings,
then let go.
Let go.

Chapter Two

Tears are the silent language of grief.
—Voltaire

Emotions

In everyday life, humans can experience a myriad of emotions across a wide spectrum. And there are many people who try to avoid emotion for fear of showing weakness, falling apart, or losing control. Some people are just plain unaware of their emotions because of early conditioning or because they are more other-focused and thus unaware of their own feelings and needs. Humans also tend to label some emotions as "good" and some as "bad." Yet, if we believe that we are made in the image and likeness of God, then *all* of our emotions are a spiritual gift from God. I like to imagine that our feelings are like a rainbow, a spectrum that colors our lives as a rainbow colors the sky. If any one color is denied or erased, the rainbow is incomplete, and its vibrancy diminished. As we explore the emotions that are a product of loss, let us view them as sacred, as holy expressions of the love we have for those people and situations over which we grieve.

There are so many emotions that are part of grief that no single model can encompass them all. Nor have I found that these emotions come in any particular order. As I mentioned in Chapter 1, sometimes *all* of the emotions can occur in the span of a single day. I will talk about these emotions individually, but they often mingle together in a stew of feelings to the point that it can be difficult to sort them out or name them all. The most important thing to remember is that *whatever* a grieving person is feeling is acceptable and normal. There is no emotion that is wrong when it comes to grief. These emotions are not listed in any particular order, other than that shock is often the first thing one feels—except when it isn't.

Shock

Many people feel shock, stunned disbelief and/or numbness at the death of a loved one, even when it was expected, and in some cases longed for. That transition from life to death is a drastic shift in one's reality, and it can be overwhelming, compromising our ability to cope. One moment the person is here, the next they are gone. In a split second, the life energy of this person no longer exists on an earthly plane. We often meet those moments with disbelief, denial, and shock.

For example, my father was a man of vital energy even in his later years. He had been an avid snow skier, golfer and outdoorsman, and his personality was larger than life. When I went to view his body at the nursing home after his death, he looked like he had just fallen asleep, something he had often done while watching television in his easy chair. There was a light breeze coming from an open window and ruffling his hospital gown so that it looked as if he was still breathing. Such was his life force that for a moment, I could almost believe he was just sleeping. It wasn't until I touched his cold feet that I knew for sure he was gone.

The shock of death is especially intense when the loved one is young and healthy or dies very suddenly. Eileen, the mother of a thirty-one-year-old son, was in total disbelief when hospital staff called to inform her that her son was suffering from sudden and catastrophic liver failure. She spent the next three days in his hospital room before he died thinking, "This can't be happening. It isn't real." The same is true of people who receive a visit from the state police informing them of a family member's death in an auto accident. It takes time for such a sudden and brutal loss to sink in.

A dear friend of mine phoned me one morning in the midst of the pandemic to tell me that her husband had literally dropped dead the night before while visiting family, presumably of a heart attack. Her constant refrain was "I don't even know." She was clearly overwhelmed by this sudden loss. The shock was such that she was incapable of even thinking about what she should do next, how she could possibly cope with the enormity of this loss. This ordinarily competent woman suddenly found that her ability to function or make plans was gone. She was utterly lost. Fortunately, her two adult daughters were with her, and even though they were also stunned by this tragedy, they were able to support their mother and help her prioritize what needed to be done. The three women stopped by my house two days later on their way home, and again, her first words were, "I don't even know. . .."

Sorrow

Sorrow has many synonyms—heartache, despair, anguish, pain, sadness, devastation. It is a deep, deep pain that sometimes manifests as a literal ache in your chest. It's what breaks you down into a quivering mass, unable to move or breathe, unable to imagine a time when it doesn't hurt this much. This kind of pain crushes you, makes you feel that you can't go on. You cry and cry and cry until you don't think you have any tears left, and then you cry some more. In the book of Psalms, David describes this feeling all too well, "Be merciful to me, Lord, for I am faint; O Lord, heal me, for my bones are in agony. How long, O Lord, how long? . . . I am worn out from groaning; all night long I flood my bed with weeping and drench my couch with tears. My eyes grow weak with sorrow." (Psalm 6:2-3, 6-7a, NIV)

The woman who lost her wife to brain cancer described her sorrow this way, "My future is a black hole." A friend whose only son was killed in a car accident cried daily for six full weeks and told me, "A part of me died that day." Sometimes, when there is this much pain, some might wonder if it will ever stop. But somehow, both of these women have, over time, come to a place of weaving their loss into the story of their lives and gone on. The pain eased bit by bit, until it was no longer crippling.

I am weary with my moaning; every night I flood my bed with tears; I drench my couch with my weeping. My eyes waste away because of grief. (Psalm 6:6-7a, NRSV)

As much as we would like to eliminate our pain or blunt our sorrow, it is virtually impossible to do, nor would it be healthy. It is important to remember that the depth of our grief is a measure of the love we have for those we lost. Consider these words from the Lebanese poet and painter, Kahlil Gibran:

> Your joy is your sorrow unmasked. And the selfsame well from which your laughter rises was oftentimes filled with your tears. And how else can it be? The deeper that sorrow carves into your being, the more joy you can contain. Is not the cup that holds your wine the very cup that was burned in the potter's oven? And is not the lute that soothes your spirit, the very wood that was hollowed with knives?
>
> When you are joyous, look deep into your heart and you shall find it is only that which has given you sorrow that is giving you joy. When you are sorrowful look again in your heart, and you shall see that in truth you are weeping for that which has been your delight.[7]

Loneliness

When someone close to you dies, it opens up a huge hole in your life. Some days the loneliness is almost more than you can bear. If your loved one shared a home with you, suddenly you are aware of silence echoing through empty halls. You wake up to the absence of the person who

[7] Gibran, *The Prophet,* p. 32-33

shared your bed. Or something happens in your day that you want to share with your loved one; you pick up the phone, and halfway through dialing you realize they're not going to answer your call. You see something in a store that your best friend would love, but they are no longer alive to receive your gift. You keep your spouse's favorite chair because it holds wonderful memories, but it also reminds you daily that they are gone.

About a year after her wife died, Jean had to sell the home they had shared. The house was just too full of memories, both the wonderful, loving ones, and the ones of her wife's last painful weeks in a hospital bed in their living room. It felt to her like the house itself kept her so immersed in death that she was unable to move on. The loneliness was just too overwhelming. Moving to a new home with a peaceful view and no agonizing memories helped her begin to heal. However, this is not true for everyone. Some people find that having reminders of their loved one, whether a piece of furniture, the outgoing message on the telephone, or a well-used piece of clothing gives them a sense of comfort and a feeling that the deceased person is still with them.

In the final two years of my mother-in-law's life, she was mostly confined to her chair in the corner of the living room. Even though my father-in-law rearranged a few things to clear out the clutter of her necessary medical paraphernalia after she died, he left her chair right where it was, draping a favorite afghan over the back and perching her special hat on the arm. He would frequently talk to her as if she were still sitting there and never failed to say goodnight to her. This gave him deep comfort and helped to ease the loneliness of her absence.

Anger

Based on my fourteen years as a mental health counselor, I think anger is the emotion humans are most conflicted about. They fear anger from others, they try to suppress it in themselves, or they feel angry all the time and lash out at the slightest provocation. Anger is one of those emotions that is often characterized as "bad" and makes us resistant to acknowledging it. The Bible is full of admonitions against anger, inducing guilt when it rises in us. Yet, if we are indeed created in the image of God, and God gets angry at times, then anger is a legitimate part of the spectrum of emotion and an acceptable expression of our humanity. Anger is just an emotion. It is neither good nor bad. In a sense, it is an emotional alarm system. Anger functions as the emotional equivalent of a fever. A fever tells us that something is wrong with our body. Anger tells us that there is something wrong in our life. I think we often confuse anger with aggression, and there lies the problem. But if we look to God as an example of how to express anger, we may be able to give ourselves permission to feel anger and then handle that anger in a godly way. There are six times in scripture that assure us, "God is slow to anger and abounding in steadfast love." This can be a guide for us in learning how to handle our own anger in healthy rather than harmful ways.

When anger is part of the grief experience, however, it complicates things. This anger can be a pervasive anger at the world, or specifically aimed at health care providers who one perceives as not having done enough to save their loved one, family members who didn't handle the loss or the aftermath in the way one expected or hoped, or people who are blamed for contributing to the death in some way. Some might be angry at themselves for perceived failures in caregiving or in their overall relationship with their lost loved one. Often, people are angry at God, which is perfectly acceptable (See Chapter Six). But in my opinion, the most difficult to accept is when the anger is directed at the person who died. It creates an internal conflict between anger and guilt that is difficult to overcome. We may feel anger over past hurts that haven't been resolved, but it seems wrong to be angry at a time when the focus is on grieving. Societal norms would have us believe that it isn't nice to criticize the dead. And yet, we do.

My friend Julia, whose husband died suddenly, acknowledged to me that she was angry at him for not taking better care of himself following an earlier heart episode. He had failed to follow doctors' orders about a healthy diet and regular exercise, and he also drank alcohol to excess. The woman whose son died of liver failure was angry at him for his years of alcohol and drug abuse, and her husband was angry at the friends who facilitated his addictions and at himself for his failure to prevent it from happening. All of these emotions create a complicated stew that pulls us down into the vortex of our conflicting feelings. We might wonder if it will ever stop. And in the meantime, we have to give ourselves permission to feel it all, even the anger.

Anger is the emotional equivalent of a fever that tells us something is wrong in our life.

Guilt

During a class on grief I was leading for a local church, the father I mentioned in the previous paragraph shared his deep guilt over his son's death. He felt that he should have done more to get his son into rehab or attend AA meetings with him or just monitor him more closely. I could see that this guilt was eating him alive. One of my favorite ways of helping clients address their often-unjustified guilt feelings is to go through an exercise I call Responsibility Pie. I draw a large circle and ask the person to name other people or situations that might have contributed to the guilt-inducing event. Then I ask how much of the responsibility that person should bear, expressed in a percentage. So, we went through this process with Dwayne listing his son, his son's friends, the girlfriend, and the doctors who had failed to recognize his son's condition sooner. As each was named, I marked off a section of the circle on the white board based on the assigned percentage. When he was done, the pie was full. I looked at him, and then at the diagram and said, "There's no room for you!" Dwayne looked stunned. All he could say was, "Oh!" From that moment on, his wife and their friends reported that he had become a different person. He seemed lighter, and the burden of guilt he had carried for so long disappeared.

Guilt is almost universally part of the grief process, especially when someone we love dies suddenly and unexpectedly. We almost always have regrets about the things we did or didn't do, the rifts we failed to mend, the things we didn't say. We all believe we will have more time. A former co-worker of my husband who had struggled with alcoholism for many years and had been in and out of rehab ultimately took his own life. My husband had attended AA meetings with this friend and co-worker, personally driven him to a rehab facility on two different occasions and visited him while he was there.

Eventually our friend lost his job due to his drinking, and we heard that he was back in rehab. A year or so later, I attended a touring performance of a Broadway show, and when the lights came up at the end, I looked across the crowded auditorium and saw our friend standing there. Anxious to get home, I chose not to go over and say hello. A few months later when we got the news of his suicide, I immediately felt guilty for not fighting through the crowds to speak to this troubled man. I wondered if I could somehow have made a difference, made him feel less alone, and prevented him from taking his life. It took me some time to realize that even if I had been able to reach him before he left the building, a few words of casual greeting would not have touched the darkness he was living with. I couldn't have foreseen what he would do a few months later or that it was the last time I would see him alive.

I have heard many stories of people whose loved ones were dying a slow and excruciating death who prayed for the end to come soon. Another client of mine was forced to make the impossible decision to end life support for her father who had fallen several stories in a work-related accident. She was only twenty years old at the time. All of these people felt deep guilt for praying that God would end their loved ones' suffering, but I imagine that most of us would do the same in that situation. We would do almost anything to relieve a loved one's suffering and pain, and that level of compassion is evidence of their love, not something to be condemned or judged. Guilt is something to be examined realistically, in light of all the factors involved, and then released.

Fear and Anxiety

When you lose someone who has been a significant figure in your life, particularly a spouse, significant other, or parent, it is natural to experience fear and/or anxiety. These are the people that are an integral part of your life, who performed specific tasks in the synergy of the relationship. Losing someone you relied on to fulfill certain functions can be terrifying. Who will do that now? Am I capable of performing these necessary tasks? For those who have lost spouses, the jobs associated just with erasing their loved one's existence from banks, Social Security, charge cards, insurance companies and so on is an enormous burden that continually reminds you of your loss. Making decisions about whether you will stay in the home you shared, downsize, or move closer to other family members or friends is extremely stressful. You might wonder if you are even capable of making those decisions while you are still deep in grief. I almost always find it advisable, if at all possible, to try not to make such life-changing decisions for at least a full year after the loss.

A woman who was going through a divorce came to see me for therapy when her anxiety became intolerable. She was a highly dependent person, and the thought of navigating life alone seemed impossible to her. She questioned every decision she made, and thoughts of the future terrified her. And yet, she was the one who still managed their joint bank account, paid bills, cancelled services, and so on. Challenging her fears helped somewhat, but she was so entrenched in her belief that she was incapable of handling life alone that the fear and anxiety lingered for a long time.

Another woman whose son died after a lifetime of ill health couldn't stop the obsessive thoughts that plagued her. The son had been born with congestive heart failure, and his parents were told that they would be lucky if he lived past the age of two. He was twenty when he died, but the anxiety of so many hospitalizations, surgeries, and bouts of pneumonia over his lifetime, and the knowledge that every breath could be his last was overwhelming. When it became clear that he would not live much longer, she and her husband opted for a risky surgery that would give him an external artificial heart. There was only a two percent chance of survival, but it was the only remaining option. Her son lived for eight months after the surgery, giving them precious time to say goodbye, but she still wonders if they made the right decision and has a hard time shaking her excessive anxious thoughts.

We all experience anxiety at one time or another, and these obsessive thoughts are hard to expunge. Once they hijack our mind, they can easily become entrenched. It is especially difficult when the future seems frightening and overwhelming because of the loss of someone with whom you shared the nitty-gritty of life. Sometimes prayer and/or meditation can help. Deep breathing with a repeated focus word is the easiest way to meditate and doesn't require special training. Just choose a word that brings comfort and repeat it on the exhale until you start to feel a calm settle over your heart and mind. This might need to be practiced several times a day at first but should eventually help your thoughts settle with just a short pause to focus on your breath. There are many scripture passages that speak to our fears as well. Some of these include Psalm 62:5-6, Lamentations 3:22-23, and Psalm 142:1-3. Should your anxious thoughts continue despite your efforts at prayer and meditation, it might be time to seek out a competent therapist or spiritual director to help you during this difficult aspect of the grief journey.

God is our refuge and strength, an ever-present help in trouble. Therefore we will not fear, though the earth give way . . ." (Psalm 46:1-2a, NIV)

Depression

It is not uncommon for deep grief to sometimes descend into clinical depression. If someone who has experienced a painful loss begins to struggle with chronic depressed mood, apathy, lack of interest or pleasure in formerly enjoyable activities, sleeping issues, significant weight loss or gain, fatigue or loss of energy, low self-esteem, poor concentration, and/or recurring thoughts of death, it is highly probable that they are dealing with some level of depression. This does not mean that there is something wrong with them or that they are not grieving "right." Grief is a heavy burden, and the circumstances are different for everyone. Depression can strike anyone depending on a myriad of circumstances. Some people are actually born with a predisposition for depression, and when enough stressors are present, the depression will manifest itself. There are many complicating factors in some losses that can lead to a depressive episode. I will address some of these factors in the next chapter on complicated grief. But even with an expected or natural death, depression can still be present depending on other life experiences, personality, et cetera.

A former client sought therapy after her husband's sudden death. He had been suffering with a number of health issues for some time, and she had been his primary caregiver as well as the one who took care of almost all household tasks and the parenting of their teenage son. Her husband had been slowly deteriorating, but there was no immediate crisis on the day that they returned home from running some errands. Her husband went to lie down for a rest while she began to prepare dinner. When the meal was ready, she went in to wake him and found him dead. By the time she came to me for help, she was already in a deep depression, virtually non-functional and incapable of performing the most minor of tasks. Her son was now routinely late for school because she was unable to get out of bed soon enough to get him there. He was having to fend for himself for meals, and the bills were going unpaid. After having to carry the weight of all the household tasks for so long, her mind and body just shut down. She was troubled by recurring dreams of finding her husband's body and was tormented by the fact that she had not been able to say goodbye or tell him "I love you" one more time. It helped her some for me to lead her through a guided imagery of saying good-bye and sharing tender words with her husband as he left this earthly life, but ultimately, she needed to begin a course of anti-depressants before the depression began to ease and she could function more normally again.

Susan's Story

Susan grew up in a church that focused on sin to the point that she felt God was always keeping score. With parents who weren't particularly affectionate, she began to believe that she was defective in some way, that nobody could possibly love her. And then along came Matty. Matty was Susan's nephew, and they had a very special bond. When he was two, he was diagnosed with leukemia, and she was by his side throughout his treatment, through all the ups and downs. He went into remission at age five but suffered a stroke three years later. Susan was the person Matty could talk to about what was happening, sometimes asking her "Am I going to die?" Wanting her nephew to have as many happy experiences as possible, she served as camp nurse so that he could attend summer church camp. This and many other life events led Matty to ask Susan once, "Why do you love me so much?" She and her husband had never had children, but it was more than that. Susan would tell you that she and Matty were soul mates, pure and simple. And then the worst-case scenario happened. Matty was diagnosed with an inoperable brain tumor. He died just before he turned twelve.

Susan entered into a darkness that was so deep, she didn't believe she would ever find her way out of it. Her grief was overwhelming, crashing over her like never-ending tidal waves. She trudged through her days like a zombie wondering how on earth she was going to go on without her beloved Matty. Then, one Sunday morning out of the blue, Susan felt compelled to go to church. There was a Methodist church just down the street, so she went. The pastor was a woman named Jane, who somehow detected Susan's pain and reached out to her with the healing grace of God. Susan continued to attend church over the following weeks and months, and Jane continued to support her in her grief. However, when Thanksgiving rolled around, Susan's husband had to be away for a business trip, and she was alone in the house. She remembers sitting on their bed, feeling utterly alone and without hope. She longed to be with Matty, and the pain was more than she could bear. She pulled her husband's gun out of a drawer and cradled it in her hands, dredging up the courage to end her life. And then the image of her friend Jane appeared before her. Susan suddenly knew she couldn't let Jane down in that way. She put away the gun and chose life.

Over time, the depression gradually waned as Susan became involved with the grief group Compassionate Friends. She began to view her year of grief as a circle rather than a path, and she was in the middle, watching her soul become whole. She felt God's presence accompanying her on this journey, and ultimately felt led to attend graduate school to obtain a master's degree in clinical psychology with an emphasis on grief. As years passed, she and Jane became best friends, and through that relationship and a deepening sense of God's love for her, she came to understand that she was a beloved child of God, not the flawed individual she had always believed herself to be.

And then she received a phone call from Jane. "Susan, I need you." Jane had been diagnosed with cancer and had only days or weeks to live. Susan immediately went to her friend and stayed by her side for thirteen days until Jane's death. Though deeply saddened by this loss, Susan celebrated the relationship that had changed her life. She was able to look back and see that God had been with her all the time, leading her toward the gradual unfolding of a life that was filled with love. She will always love Matty and Jane and knows that they walk with her as she remains open to the journey of grief and the new places it will take her.

Confusion

Sometimes people experience a time of confusion and lack of direction. It's almost as though the wheels have come off the bus, nothing makes sense anymore, and we don't know what to do next.

Melissa's husband's abandonment of her and their children was beyond her comprehension. She couldn't fathom why he chose to leave the marriage so abruptly, leaving her to fend for herself. Their marriage hadn't been perfect by any means, but she had thought they were trying to make it work. They had made a vow to one another, lived together for years, and then he just walked away. What would she do now? How could she handle seminary and a job while taking care of her three children, cooking, cleaning, and helping with homework? It was all just too much, and she had no idea where to start. Ultimately, she was able to accept the loss and move on, clarify her priorities, and discover a life of meaning and purpose for herself and her children, but it was a hard road with many bumps along the way.

A friend of mine who was ordinarily capable and self-confident found herself floundering after her father died. They hadn't had a great relationship, and he had been fairly dictatorial. Even though Chris was in her late forties, she still felt that her father's dictums from childhood were a constant reminder that she was not living up to his expectations. After his death, she felt rudderless, even though her conscious mind knew that it was permissible to choose a gentler path. It took some time for her to trust in herself and move in a healthier direction. She could view her father in a new way, see him clearly, understanding his past and the events that shaped his personality, while choosing a different approach in her own life. Eventually, she learned to love him without the burden of his own pain which he had projected onto others.

Relief

If you have ever watched a loved one suffer the indignities and pain of a long, slow, and painful death, you have probably met the end of their struggle with a measure of relief. The mother whose son was born with serious heart issues that necessitated a life of hospitalizations and surgeries spent twenty years preparing herself for his death. Though devastating, when his death finally came, she felt a significant measure of relief. Her son was no longer in pain.

She no longer went to sleep waiting for the phone to ring, waiting for the next health crisis. Yet she grieved his loss deeply. The hole her son's death left in her life was huge, and there were many times when she fell into it. Now, after four years, she doesn't fall in anymore, but sometimes she says she just sits on the edge.

So many people I know have witnessed the lingering death of aging parents with dementia or the suffering of family members or friends with cancers that cause intense pain, severe bleeding, loss of bladder or bowel control, and/or embarrassing procedures that make the patient feel less than human. In those situations, there is an almost universal relief that the pain and struggle are over when their loved ones die. This does not diminish their grief in any way, nor is it uncaring or selfish. This kind of relief is born of love, of the realities of watching their loved ones suffer and praying that their pain might be ended.

Spiritual Practice

If we are created in the image and likeness of God, then all of our emotions are a part of who God is and who we are. There are no "bad" emotions. Imagine emotions as a rainbow. If you take any particular emotion and try to suppress it, part of the rainbow is missing. It loses its vibrancy. It is nearly impossible to suppress one emotion without dimming the others. Reflect on all the emotions you have experienced as a part of your grief. Can you give yourself the grace to accept them all, recognize them as a pathway to healing, and be grateful for them, even the painful ones?

Prayer

Beloved, thank you for the gift of emotions that color our lives like a rainbow. Help us recognize them as a reflection of your love for us, your provision that allows us to crawl out of the morass of grief onto solid ground. When we are in sorrow, give us the memory of joy. When we are in pain, help us feel the comfort of your arms holding us as a mother holds her weeping child. When we are feeling angry or guilty, help us receive your understanding, for you know from whence it comes, and you know that healing will make its way into our hearts in good time. Amen.

Interlude

Still
You lost her,
and I know
how it stripped you
of your defenses,
emptied you out,
making a hollow
in which your pain
echoed against
the walls of it.
She was your home,
the only safe place
you ever knew.
You feel as though
you are homeless now,
wandering in the desert,
exiled from her love,
alone.
Do you not know?
She is still holding you
with a love
not limited by time
or space,
still singing to you
in the silences of the night,
still sheltering you
in the shadow of her memory.
She is still your home,
not with walls and doors

but with a love
that transcends
our earthly understandings
and whispers,
I loved you before,
I love you now,
I love you
still.

Chapter 3

Complicated Grief

Deliver me from my enemies, O my God;
Protect me from those who rise up against me.
Psalm 59:1 (NRSV)

It would be easy to assume that the term "complicated grief" implies that there is such a thing as "simple grief." Nothing could be farther from the truth! Grief is always hard, always painful, but there are some situations that make it even harder to navigate the detours onto which loss leads you. Perhaps the above quote from Psalms might help to clarify somewhat. I think we can all identify with the psalmist a bit—not specifically being besieged by literal enemies, but feeling besieged by the painful, stressful, or negative events that take you to the outer limits of your ability to function or cope.

Sometimes, however, the enemies are real. As one man's wife lay dying of incurable brain cancer, her adult children were making his life hell. They didn't approve of him abiding by his wife's wishes to bring in hospice care and went to extreme measures in an attempt to thwart him. The son and daughter weren't ready to lose their mother and plotted to get him out of the home so they could "save" her. They went so far as to call the police and claim that their stepfather was abusing his wife. The anger he felt at their actions made his grief a tornado of mixed emotions.

One of the situations that might plunge you into complicated grief is a sudden or untimely death. Death at the end of a natural life span is far different than the death of a child with a fatal disease or an adult who is struck down by a heart attack or a horrific accident. Another factor in complicated grief is when someone experiences multiple grief events in close proximity. Looking back on the cluster of painful circumstances my husband and I experienced during the first year of the pandemic, it's no wonder I was such a wreck!

A woman I know lost her 30-year-old son when he was hit by a car a few years ago. This threw her into an ocean of grief that her husband (not the son's natural father) just couldn't handle. The couple separated at a time when the mother, who had been preparing for the ministry, changed her church affiliation due to issues unrelated to her loss and began the ordination process in another denomination. Add to this the fact that she was also still receiving periodic treatments for her own recurring cancer. When you consider the "piling on" of all these losses, it's no wonder that her grieving journey took what seemed like eternity. She became like a zombie, going through the motions of life on autopilot, sleeping little, crying almost non-stop for weeks, unable to return to work for three full months after her son's death. It took her two years before she really felt like she had begun to heal. Despite the return of "normal" functioning, she says, "The loss of a child never goes away. It may subside for a while, but it is always there."

Sudden losses are always particularly hard to make sense of. I'm reminded of my friend whose husband literally dropped dead while supervising the clean-up crew following his stepfather's suicide. He had had heart issues a few years prior, but there had been no indication of ongoing issues, so when my friend received the news, she felt completely lost. I wrote the following reflection the day after his funeral:

> Bill's funeral was yesterday, so many people there broken-hearted at his untimely death, thrust suddenly into this strange land called Grief. They arrived there blinking, frightened, torn asunder from the life they once knew, experiencing whiplash from the impact, the shattering jolt of death. How does one navigate this unknown territory? Well-meaning people hand out road maps, but they're like foreign words on the page. The signposts don't match what we see, what we feel. It's like our compass is spinning wildly out of control; our GPS is speaking in a foreign tongue. How do we deal with this pain, the agony that cripples us, brings us to our knees? Is there no comfort? Is there no hope, no relief from the pain, no guide in this alien terrain? Only this—stay where you are until you feel the

> strength for just one step. Breathe, cry, curse the heavens. Remember. Pray. Take another step. Repeat. Eventually the steps will come more often. Eventually you'll stand up straighter. Eventually this strange new world will take on the contours of something that looks like home.

The thing that struck me during that time of remembering was how many people had been impacted by Bill's life, how much they loved him. The ultimate truth is that love abides, that our loved ones will live on in our memories forever.

Another factor in complicated grief is when feelings about the deceased person were ambivalent at best or even primarily negative. A fellow therapist's mother was cold and incapable of showing affection. She considered her social relationships more important than her children and grandchildren. Her hugs were stiff and without warmth. When she died at the age of 98, my friend was surprised by her grief, not about her mother's loss, but for the loss of a relationship that never was, that she had longed for her entire life. So many people expressed condolences to my friend, assuming that she must be missing her mother terribly, and those sentiments just deepened her grief at not having the kind of mother other people had. She felt very alone in her grief, because so few people understood what she was really feeling. And she was envious of all these people whose cards and phone calls indicated that they had

had mothers who were everything she had longed for and never received.

Another woman's mother was an alcoholic, and as the eldest girl in the family, my friend ended up being parentified, serving as a mother surrogate to her younger siblings. This led to strained relations between the two, especially when the daughter was awarded guardianship of her mother. When the mother died, it was a relief more than anything, and there were a lot of "leftover emotions" that she had to deal with in the aftermath. Fortunately, she had good friends who helped her through that difficult time.

Peter's Story

Peter grew up with a narcissistic father, Jack, who was verbally and occasionally physically abusive to both his children and his wife, Peter's mother. Jack was critical and demeaning, which led to Peter's tendency to doubt himself and seek approval from others. As with most narcissistic fathers, Jack placed all his expectations on his son, hoping he would follow in his footsteps and become an engineer. When Peter decided to enter the ministry instead, Jack was furious and tried in every way possible to dissuade Peter from his chosen profession. He frequently complained that "the church took you away from me." As an adult, Peter became increasingly frustrated with his dad's manipulations and tried to distance himself, but this just led to harassing phone calls that left him hurt and angry. Every attempt at holding clear boundaries made his father more determined to draw Peter back into his gravitational pull.

Things worsened when Peter's mother finally decided to end the marriage. Jack's behavior immediately went into overdrive. Phone calls to Peter increased as Jack attempted to re-establish contact and bring Peter over to his side. The turmoil continued until Peter finally cut off all ties with his dad. He changed his cell phone number, but church phone numbers are easy to find, and Jack would often call Peter at work. Every time Peter was re-appointed to a new church (which happens every few years in the Methodist church), he purposefully kept that information from his father, but Jack managed to find him anyway and called the church again and again in his attempts to restore communication.

In order to be able to cash his wife out in the division of property, Jack was forced to sell a number of assets, including the family motor home. When her attorney and an assistant went to pick it up from Jack, a small explosive device went off when they started the engine. No one was injured, but it was clear that Jack had rigged it out of spite. This started a downward spiral that ultimately led to mental illness, dementia, and an involuntary admission into a mental facility and then, as his health declined, a nursing home. When Peter and his sister went to their dad's house to clear it out, they found piles and piles of junk, numerous guns, and many valuable items that had not been listed as assets in the divorce settlement—all clear evidence of Jack's long slide into paranoia.

Ultimately, there came a time when Jack deteriorated to the point that he was placed in hospice care. Peter's sister called to let him know, and he went to see his father one last time. He had a flickering hope that he would be recognized, that his father would express regret for the long years of emotional abuse, but that was not to be. Peter spent an entire night at Jack's bedside, but he never regained consciousness and slipped away the next morning.

How does one feel when the person you have been battling your entire life is gone? It wasn't shock or disbelief as the experts will tell you, but a cauldron of many things. Relief that this man who had stalked him for so many years was gone. Anger at all he had been put through. Sadness that there had been no recognition of inappropriate behavior, no apology, no acknowledgement of the pain he had caused. And then, over time, came a growing confidence, a release of the anxiety of waiting for the next phone call, the next outrageous act, the next shoe to drop. Gone too, was a piece of Peter's identity. He was no longer Jack's son. If there was sorrow, it was sorrow over what he had never had, a father who genuinely loved him or recognized him as an individual in his own right instead of as an offshoot of Jack's own ego.

Underlying mental illness can be another factor in complicated grief. Recall the woman I mentioned in Chapter 2 whose husband's sudden death propelled her into a deep depression that left her unable to function. Sometimes an inherited tendency toward anxiety can make the stresses of loss and the to-do list of death particularly difficult. In any close relationship, there is an interdependency that develops over time. This can be true, not only of couples, but of parents and adult children, siblings, close friends, et cetera. Tasks and responsibilities are shared based on the particular gifts of each person in the relationship. When one partner dies, the tasks they had performed fall on the other to take care of. The survivor suddenly has to figure out when to get the oil changed or the tires rotated or how to cook a healthy meal or clean the toilets or balance the checkbook. When that person has anxiety, life becomes a series of seemingly insurmountable challenges.

In some cases, grief gets delayed for any number of reasons—the demands of settling an estate, work-related issues, the illness of another family member, et cetera. When my mother-in-law died, my husband had to plunge into the tasks of helping his dad dispose of all her medications and the equipment that had been keeping her alive, making burial arrangements, and so on. He then dropped his father off at the hospital for surgery to remove a cancerous kidney before driving back home. The three-hour drive was his only chance to grieve, and he cried the whole way. Once home, he busied himself with notifying all the banks, insurance companies and Social Security of his mother's death. He developed a cough and a headache, which he assumed was a cold he caught from his father. He finally decided he'd better get checked for COVID, and he tested positive. He called the hospital where his dad was recovering from surgery and told them to test him. Sure enough, he was also positive and very ill with COVID pneumonia. They whisked him to the COVID floor immediately, but his condition was serious. The following days were filled with phone calls to doctors, family members, and his dad, never sure if that would be the last time we spoke with him. At some point, the tide turned, and he was able to go home but needed round-the-clock care.

My sister-in-law and my husband took turns nursing him back to health, but it was several weeks before he was truly out of the woods. It wasn't until we had my mother-in-law's burial service a month later that any of us could truly begin to grieve her loss.

Cody's Story

Cody and his dad were best friends. His dad worked selling airplane conversions, and aviation was in their blood. Every weekend or school holiday the two of them were at the local airfield building an airplane they would eventually fly together. One day, when Cody was 39, he heard a news alert that there had been a plane crash near the airfield where his dad worked. He texted his dad to get the scoop on what happened but got no answer. He called his mom to see if she had heard anything, and when she answered in the negative, he instinctively drove to her house with a sense of foreboding. He had just arrived when his mom got a call stating that her husband and their company's test pilot had been in an accident and that his father was currently en route to the hospital. It wasn't until Cody and his mom arrived at the hospital that they were informed that both his dad and the other pilot had perished in the accident. Death had been instantaneous.

His mother fell apart at first and then became virtually catatonic. She didn't want to see her husband's body, so Cody left her in the waiting room so he could see his father one last time. He didn't cry, couldn't cry. Cody was the oldest of four kids, and every time his dad had left on a business trip, he had told Cody, "You've gotta step up while I'm away. Take care of things for me." And now,

Cody could almost hear his dad again saying, "You've gotta step up." And so he was already creating a check list in his mind of things that had to be done and who he could delegate to do them. He was the big brother, the one who stood outside the family dysfunction and held things together. He knew that this was no time for grieving. The only time he really broke down was during the "missing man" flight formation at the airfield where they held the memorial service two weeks later. Cody had collapsed in a corner of the hangar and fallen apart. Then he got back up, brushed off his pants and stepped back into the fray.

For two weeks, Cody continued to take care of all the details that need attending when a loved one dies. When he finally went back to work, he found that he had been promoted to a new position, which required training and adjustment to the new situation. He also had to monitor his mother's spending as she plowed through the unexpected windfall from his dad's life insurance policy. There was no time for grief then either. Life became "white noise" for a long time. He was numb, just going through the motions. He dated a lot of different women just to put a band aid on the loneliness he felt at the loss of his best friend.

In the meantime, the wife of the test pilot who had also died in the wreck was researching how it could have happened. Eventually, she found answers which led her to ask Cody to join her in a lawsuit against the firm who had done a repair incorrectly and thus caused the crash. This plunged him into another busy time of consulting with lawyers, signing affidavits, plotting strategy, and being interviewed by local news reporters. Again, no time for grief.

Then three years after the accident, Cody began dating the woman who would become his wife. She was stable, supportive, and empathetic. She helped him understand that the world didn't have to rest on his shoulders, that he could let go and begin to truly grieve. He was able to let tears come then, let his emotions find expression. He had been angry at God for letting this happen, even doubting God's existence for a while. But his wife helped him with this too in her capacity as an ordained pastor. He understands now that God does not intentionally cause our suffering but walks with us as we go through the travails of life.

Cody had come a long way on his journey of grief when he crashed his own plane with his father-in-law in the passenger seat. Both survived with relatively minor injuries, but the emotional impact was huge. He felt extreme guilt for putting his father-in-law's life in danger, for wrecking the plane that he and his father had built together, for the mistake that brought the plane down. He wondered why he had survived but his father hadn't. And then the anger reared its ugly head. He freely admits that he externalized this anger for a while, taking it out on the people he loved. But gradually, through the full expression of a swirling mass of emotion, Cody began to heal, and the tide of grief started to ebb. Life began to feel manageable again. Of course, as with most of us who've experienced loss, there are still times when he misses his father intensely, when he shuts down to avoid the pain and defaults to living on auto pilot.

This is only a brief examination of all the possible factors that might contribute to complicated grief, and what might be causational for one person might not be for another. So many factors that make us who we are play into how we respond to death and trauma—stressful life stages, early childhood experiences, the level of relationship, innate coping skills or lack thereof, the type of loss— that it would be impossible to predict how anyone might respond to the death of a loved one.

Spiritual Practice

Life is complicated. Death and loss make it even more so. Sometimes we just don't have the wherewithal to handle it well. We struggle. We stumble. We wonder how we will go on. And sometimes we castigate ourselves for not doing better, for not coping, for not "getting over it." Examine your expectations of yourself. Are those expectations reasonable? Challenge the inner critic that causes you pain, and let harmful expectations go. Be gentle with yourself. Forgive yourself for the feelings and actions that aren't a reflection of your best self. Treat yourself gently. Ask for help. Practice self care. Your lost loved one is worthy of your grief, so let yourself grieve in your own way and in your own time.

Prayer

Gracious God, you know our every thought and feeling. You know all the ways in which our grief is impacted by the complications of our lives, the wounds we carry, the losses we have experienced. Sometimes we feel like we can't go on. Every step feels like we are wearing concrete shoes. Each morning feels like a re-awakening of loss. Like the psalmists, we have lain in our beds in the dark of night, flooding our pillow with our tears and our groaning. Hear us, O Lord. Give us comfort. Bring people into our lives to lift us up when we fall, when we feel we cannot go on even another hour. Even though the pain is unbearable, help us remember that we are on holy ground and that you walk with us every step of the way. Amen.

Interlude

What If?
What if
love was mixed
with a lifetime of wounding?
What if
grief was mixed
with regret, anger, relief?
What if no one understood?
What if you felt
nothing at all?
What if the grieving
wasn't about what you lost
but about what you never had?
What if you give yourself
permission
to be honest with yourself,
forgive yourself
for what you don't feel,
for what you didn't do?
What if you let go?
Walk on.
Leave your baggage
by the side of the road..

Chapter 4

Woes of the World

Whether or not we consciously recognize it, the daily diminishment of species, habitats, and cultures is noted in our psyches. Much of the grief we carry is not personal, but shared, communal. . .. It takes everything we have to deny the sorrows of the world.[8]

While we have been primarily discussing our personal and private losses, larger communal losses also take their toll on us. These are the events that make the front page of the newspapers and hit us like a tsunami with their impact on our communities, our nation, our world. Russia invades Ukraine, and we are sickened by the cruelty and lust for power. Most of us remember where we were when terrorists flew jets into the twin towers and the Pentagon, leaving hundreds of people dead and thousands with traumatic memories that will haunt them forever. Far too often children are mown down in their own classrooms by a disaffected gunman who is mad at the world. LGBTQ individuals are targeted in gay nightclubs where they should have been able to feel safe. Buildings collapse, killing hundreds because someone cut corners in the

---

[8] Weller, *The Wild Edge of Sorrow,* p. 46

construction process. Innocent children are ripped from their parents' arms and put in cages at the border. Governments crumble under the weight of their own hubris. Then there are the societal ills of racism, anti-gay sentiment, religious persecution, political upheaval, poverty, homelessness, and other issues that stir up dissent and often end in protests that take lives and destroy property. Summer after summer, the western United States are on fire. Drastic weather events destroy everything in their wake. The ice cap is melting, and the oceans are rising. Climate change is a threat to our planet and everyone who lives on it.

These events, which impact all our lives, invoke outrage, fear, despair, sadness, deep distress, grief. We are horrified by the injustices that take the lives of the innocent. We are aggrieved by the failure of our government to act in ways that prevent these catastrophes from occurring. We are offended by the thoughtless practices of companies who put profit ahead of safety, resulting in tragic events such as the explosion on the oil rig Deep Water Horizon in 2010. We can become overwhelmed at this unending parade of human tragedy. Jeremiah expresses this well: "Since my people are crushed, I am crushed; I mourn and horror grips me. Is there no balm in Gilead? Is there no physician there? Why then is there no healing for the wound of my people? Oh, that my head were a spring of water and my eyes a fountain of tears! I would weep day and night for the slain of my people."[9]

---

[9] Jeremiah 8:21-9:1 (NIV)

We may try to push those powerful emotions aside in order to be able to function or get on with the daily business of our lives, but as we discussed in Chapter Two, we shut down our emotions at a cost. We may fast forward through distressing news stories, skim the daily paper, leave the room when people are discussing troubling issues, but it's impossible to completely shut yourself off from the disturbing events in the world. Even if we try to shut them out, they are still impacting us at a deeper level and eroding our ability to cope with everyday stressors and personal grief events.

Our Communal Story

It began as a small story on the inside pages of the newspaper—a new virus was spreading in China. We shrugged. This was nothing new, and China is far away. We'll be fine. Then we heard that there were some cases in Europe. There's still an ocean in between us. Nothing to worry about. Then came news of a smattering of cases in New York and California. Unless we were from there, we might have started feeling a little bit of anxiety, but on the whole, we weren't yet alarmed. And then, the numbers began to increase exponentially and creep closer and closer to our own communities. That's when full-fledged panic set in. Soon we were in quarantine, hiding fearfully in our homes while the government hemmed and hawed about what protocols should be established for our safety. How do you balance the desire to save lives while preserving personal liberties? At what cost?

And so it began. Isolation, businesses closed, office buildings gone dark, streets eerily empty as people scrambled to figure out how to work from home, how to navigate ZOOM or Facetime for meetings, how to pay the rent when they were laid off or flat out fired, where to find toilet paper and flour in a store of empty shelves. The news was all bad, but we couldn't turn it off. We were front row center as our elected government leaders argued about how to respond to the pandemic. We despaired as the experts changed their advice on a daily basis as they strove to learn more about this new virus. Don't wear a mask, do wear a mask. It's airborne, it's transmitted via touch. We watched as hospitals filled up with the most serious cases and medical personnel wept on live TV, begging for adequate supplies of PPEs, more help, more beds. We saw dead bodies piled on loading docks outside big city hospitals because there was no more room in the morgue. Trucks transported bodies to funeral homes that were already overloaded. We saw sons and daughters, spouses and children saying good-bye to their dying loved ones via a computer screen or peering through a window. It broke our hearts.

And during this worldwide crisis, this history-making event, we were alone and scared. We were isolated from friends, neighbors, loved ones. If we lost someone to the coronavirus, we couldn't bury them, couldn't hold a funeral, couldn't receive in-person hugs and comfort from friends, church acquaintances or our pastors. Grieving was a solo experience even though we were all experiencing the same thing. We were helpless against this monster that was killing hundreds of thousands in just our country alone.

And if we were unfortunate enough to contract this microscopic demon, the fear rose inside until it almost choked us. Spouses made sure their partners knew all the passwords, knew where the bank accounts were, knew how to reboot the computer, start the snow blower, cook a decent meal, do the laundry—all the things that one partner or the other takes on as their duties in the symbiotic relationship that is marriage. Death seemed to be right outside our door, a dark figure waiting to take us away.

Dark days require
sack cloth and ashes,
songs of lament.
God save us!
The specter of death
stalks us,
his wicked laughter
haunting our dreams.
Where is justice?
Where is healing?
Where is compassion?
Our leaders cry crocodile tears
but care nothing
for the plight of the lowly.
Where are you, O God?
Why do you remain far off?
Come near to us!
Rescue us from this invisible enemy.

We lost so much during the pandemic, it was overwhelming, and we had nowhere to go with the fear, the grief, the loneliness, the longing for normalcy. We weren't living so much as surviving, putting one foot in front of the other, going through the motions of daily life. And we wondered whether we would ever experience normalcy again.

I think many of us just became numb. We were lost in the abyss of so many emotions, we couldn't truly experience any of them in a way that released us from their grip. And so now, the task is before us. Now that the danger is mostly passed, how do we begin to address the morass of our feelings and begin to heal? How do we begin to rebuild our lives after the tornado that was COVID?

It's my belief that communal events need to be grieved communally. Notice how, after every school shooting, people gather spontaneously for a vigil, lighting candles, placing flowers and memorial objects, singing together, weeping. This is a place where the keening cries of those who mourn will be heard and honored, tears can be shed without fear of ridicule, and the collective ache of a community is lifted up. After the attacks of 9/11, churches, synagogues, and mosques held special services so people could grieve in their sanctuaries and receive words of comfort and hope from their religious leaders. When national or global tragedies strike, people often start fund drives to collect money for the victims and their families or donate to organizations that are bringing aid to those affected and/or working toward the elimination of the causes of these troubling events. Crowds march for justice, freedom, gun control, an end to racism, and other issues that trouble our world. The solidarity of people marching together allows us to feel less helpless and hopeless.

Despite its many pitfalls, Facebook can be another way in which we grieve in community. During the worst of

COVID, it was really our only way. When you posted your grief about the woes of the world, your friends and loved ones responded with virtual hugs, heart emojis, caring comments, offers of prayer, affirmations that they shared your views and were grieving too. It was and continues to be what helps us feel less alone. And for the most part, those who disagree with your views on national or worldwide issues will leave you alone rather than stirring up contention when your heart is breaking over the tragedies we witness in this wounded world.

> *"Communal lament is important for several reasons. It wakes us up, and in doing so, makes us mindful of the pain of our neighbors, who no longer can go about business as usual when the women begin to wail. Their keening rattles both marrow and bone. . . . The collective wail reminds us that we are not alone."* —Barbara Holmes

In biblical times, the Israelites gathered at the Wailing Wall to weep and wail, to cry out to God for help or ask why God allowed such horrible things to happen. Grief was also expressed through the rending of clothing or by dressing in sack cloth and covering themselves in ashes in the public square. These were outward signs of inner grief. Another way to grieve collectively is through lament. A lament is a written or oral expression of grief or sorrow.

The book of Psalms contains many psalms of lament in addition to the familiar psalms of joy and gratitude. Laments can be both personal and communal. It was through personal lament that King David cried out to God in fear of his enemies, his losses in battle, his existential loneliness, and his pain over the perceived absence of God. Communal laments mourned the loss of Israel's homeland when they were exiled by their conquerors to a foreign land, witnessed the destruction of their temple, or were subjugated by a foreign ruler. In modern times, we can lament over the communal losses we face, the many issues we have been discussing in this chapter. Richard Rohr writes: "Lament allows the pain to escape and stitches us to our neighbors. We are called to weep with those who weep and mourn with those who mourn. Our tears are our prayers when we can't speak, a baptism of sorts, a salty healing, a sign of our vulnerability, and a liturgical response to violence."[10] Below is an example of one biblical psalm of communal lament that is just as appropriate now as it was thousands of years ago:

> Help, Lord, for the godly are no more;
> the faithful have vanished from among men.
> Everyone lies to his neighbor;
> their flattering lips speak with deception.
> May the Lord cut off all flattering lips
> and every boastful tongue
> that says "We will triumph with our tongues;
> we own our lips—who is our master?"
> —Psalm 12: 1-4 (NIV)

---

[10] Rohr, Communal Lament, Center for Action & Contemplation, 7/27/2021

As you can see, the biblical laments are sometimes quite violent in their language. It can be shocking, but then, so can our own thoughts at times. The psalms let us know that there's nothing we can't say to God. It's okay to think those kinds of thoughts, knowing that we would never actually act on those feelings. We can rant to God about the injustices in the world, but we leave the justice to God and to our legal systems.

It is also helpful to write your own psalms of lament when you are feeling grief at the woes of the world or the losses in your own life. I often write my own laments when I despair of the violence, corruption, and tragedies in our world. Below is one example:

> The world can break your heart
> if you let it —
> pictures of gaunt brown children
> in Africa, bellies swollen
> with hunger, flies circling
> their heads, their eyes huge
> and hopeless—
> Families fleeing war,
> leaving everything behind
> to land on foreign shores—
> pictures of the COVID ward,
> patients alone, terrified,
> saying goodbye to loved ones
> on a 5 x 8 screen,
> untouchable except by gloved hands.
> Lost lives, lost loves,

all the things that make you cry.
The world can break your heart—
I think you should let it,
and then you can be healed.
Then light can stream through the cracks
of your brokenness—
the delighted squeal of a toddler,
a hand to hold,
the swell of heavenly music,
the light in your beloved's eyes,
the promise of dawn.

One of my favorite morning prayers begins with the words, "…new every morning is your love, great God of light, and all day long, you are working for good in the world."[11] These words give me hope—hope that the Beloved is actively working for peace and justice in this broken world. They remind me that I am not alone, that there are millions, even billions of believers trying to follow the words of Micah, to do justice, love mercy, and walk humbly with God.[12] And that God in her love for her children is moving in ways I cannot begin to comprehend and that I may never see or know. I pray that God stirs me to service, to be a part of this vast movement of love, to bring hope to the suffering children, trusting that whatever little thing I do is multiplied by God's great compassion every day, all day long.

Spiritual Practice

---

[11] Upper Room Worshipbook, p. 8

[12] Micah 6:8

Gather with safe friends who are also struggling with the woes of the world and talk freely of your grief over poverty, injustice, war, cruelty, school shootings, climate change, needless bloodshed, et cetera. Discuss small ways that you might begin to make a difference together or individually. Or work with your pastor to create a special worship service that allows for communal grieving over one or several of these issues. Remember that grief arises out of love for that which is lost, and that love abides.

Prayer

Holy and gracious God, life is such a mixed blessing. In the midst of sorrow and pain, the sun peeks through the clouds for one blindingly beautiful moment. In the midst of smiles and laughter with old friends, ominous thunder rolls. The darkness and the light are never separate from one another. Even in our grief, we can know love—conveyed by a touch, a phone call, a caring glance. When our lives are sweet, and pain seems far away, help us to remember the hurting ones, to reach out as an earthly vessel of your compassion. And when we feel swamped by the devastation of loss, help us look for the light, remembering that in the darkness of Good Friday, Easter is still coming—again and again and again. Amen.

Interlude

COVID Blessing
This blessing is everywhere now,
touching the dying and the living,
wiping sweat from the faces
of hospital personnel,
climbing into bed beside
the fevered and frightened ones,
putting arms around the grieving,
comforting the lonely.
This blessing is tired too,
but it keeps going,
reading a book
to a child whose parents
just need five minutes of peace.
This blessing keeps moving,
arms wide enough
to encompass the whole world,
to meet us where we are.

Chapter 5

Leaning Into Grief

> *"Yet there is a healing that comes in our grieving, a redemption that does something other than restore us to the lives we once knew. This healing comes, somewhat paradoxically, in allowing ourselves to give exquisite attention to our grief—to feel it in its terrible fullness instead of ignoring it, to let it speak instead of silencing it, and to allow it to show us a way that we could not find on our own."* —Jan Richardson[13]

Grief is hard. It is exhausting. Sometimes, it feels bottomless. Often, it brings us to our knees. And when we are tired, when we are overcome with the pain of grief, when we are caught up in the realities of daily living and the many tasks that are now suddenly ours to do, it is easy to forget to breathe. Not literally of course, because breathing is an involuntary body function, but the kind of deep intentional breathing that slows your heartbeat, allows

[13] Richardson, *The Cure for Sorrow: A Book of Blessings for Times of Grief,* p. 172

you to expel some of the tension in your body, be still for a moment, and pay attention to who you are, where you are, and what you are feeling. This kind of breath is holy. It allows the sacred to enter in. The Reverend Mihee Kim-Kort nudges us to "keep putting one foot in front of the other and do the sanctified work that is breathing."[14]

Intentional breathing isn't something we do naturally. Since our body breathes whether we are paying attention or not, we often fail to notice our own breath. Yet it is in times of our deepest pain that we most need to slow down, become aware of our breath, receive it as gift, and feel the peace that comes when we attend to the ebb and flow, the pauses at the top and bottom of our breath, the slowing of the heartbeat when we pay attention. This feeling can be deepened by placing your hand over your heart and noticing the weight of it, grounding you in your body and soul, releasing emotions that beg for expression in this time of deep grief.

Of course, it may be that you would prefer not to feel anything, that you want to distance yourself from your grief rather than move closer to it, that you want to suppress the emotions that are boiling inside you lest they render you incapable of functioning at all. And yet, the many emotions of grief demand expression; they will wait as long as it takes for you to tend to them. They refuse to just go away. They long for release, and they will not let you ignore them forever. One of the primary ways of releasing emotion is through your tears. Amazingly, the only way that the stress hormone cortisol is expelled from the body is through the tear ducts. When we weep, we are

---

[14] A Rhythm of Prayer, ed. Sarah Bessey, p. 37

literally ridding our body of a hormone that, when allowed to build up, is physically harmful to us.

*Jesus wept. (*John 11:35)

For some however, allowing themselves to weep openly is extremely difficult to do. In many childhood homes, crying was ridiculed, forbidden, or even punished. How many people of the Baby Boom generation, for example, were threatened with the statement, "I'll give you something to cry about!"? Tears were viewed as a sign of weakness in homes that valued stoicism and toughness. For those people, giving themselves permission to cry is virtually impossible. Even when they become aware of the deep well of tears building up inside them, they will continue to hold back for fear that if they start crying, they'll never be able to stop. And yet, Scripture is full of references to weeping and mourning. Many of them contain promises of comfort, joy, dancing, and blessings to come when the dark night of grief has passed. Time after time, we are assured that our weeping will not last forever, that our time of mourning will be followed by joy and laughter. Psalm 30:11 (NIV) declares, "You turned my wailing into dancing; you removed my sackcloth and clothed me with joy."

That word "wail" makes us a little anxious though, doesn't it? It feels more out of control than mere weeping. Have you ever heard someone wail? I remember when my mother-in-law passed away, and my father-in-law was absolutely bereft. I was talking on the phone with my husband who was driving his father to the funeral home, and I could hear him literally wailing in the background. It was a haunting cry, a sound that rose up unbidden from the core of his being. It's not a sound we usually hear in the public arena because it seems so out of control, and we are a culture that values being in control at all costs.

While wailing is seldom heard in today's society, it was perfectly acceptable in the biblical world. Mourners would often put on sackcloth, a course material made of goat's hair, as a way of showing their heartfelt sorrow over the loss of a loved one. They would weep and wail, not caring if they were in a public place or inside their home. This is the personal form of lament, and we are assured that when we pour out our souls before God in this way, we are heard and comforted. In her book *This Here Flesh,* author Cole Arthur Riley tells us, "Every howl reverberates off the walls of God's chest and finds its way back to us, carrying his own tears with it."[15]

There is something about the expelling of our grief through loud cries and moaning that releases our pain, gives it expression, and makes space inside of us for receiving the comfort of God. For at least a little while, it allows us to be emptied of our grief so that we might find the stillness that allows us to hear God speaking to our hearts.

> *"Meanwhile, the moment we get tired in the waiting, God's Spirit is right alongside helping us along. If we don't know how or what to pray, it*

[15] Riley, *This Here Flesh,* p. 99

doesn't matter. He does our praying in and for us, making prayer out of our wordless sighs, our aching groans." Romans 8:26 (MSG)

Another way in which we enter more deeply into our grief is through prayer. When we are broken-hearted, we fall into the arms of a God whose heart has been broken open for the suffering of the world. God, in Jesus, knows intimately the pathways of grief. In his book, *Tell It Slant*, Eugene Peterson says, "Catastrophe and crisis very often take us to the bedrock of our humanity, where our language is purged of pretense and piety, and we pray from the gut."[16] When we pray our grief, we let go of any illusions about what prayer ought to be, what words we should use, the proper way to address God, the idea that God will smite us if we aim some of our anger in a heavenly direction. And when no words come, we can fall back on the recitation of the Kyrie, "Lord, have mercy! God have mercy. Lord, have mercy." And when even that is more than we can manage, God hears us still. When our loss is too deep for words, God knows. God sees into our hearts and responds to the pain that is written there.

One of the ways in which I often express grief is through journaling. It helps me to put my thoughts and emotions on paper, just letting the words spill from my pencil without editing them. Many times I've written down something I hadn't even realized I was feeling or thinking until I read it on the page in front of me. My words often

[16] Peterson, *Tell It Slant*, p. 46

arrange themselves into a poem, and I offer the one below, written a year after my mother-in-law had died.

A year ago,
a dark chasm opened up,
an emptiness
that was her absence—
such a powerful force—
gone.
A gaping hole
in our hearts,
Death ripping her away—
cruel and kind
at the same time.
That hole is still here,
will always be,
but the edges
are softer now,
the ache easing,
the heart discovering
she's never really gone.

If you're already in the habit of journaling, writing your grief will come naturally for you. If you have never done so, the loss of a loved one might be a good time to try. You don't have to have a fancy notebook or a leather-bound journal or a special pen in order to start. Your writing doesn't have to be neat or even stay on the line. I use a pencil most of the time, and I've been known to scribble or write in BIG letters when that felt like the best way to express what I was feeling. Also, good grammar, spelling, and penmanship are completely optional! The only thing that matters is expressing all the different emotions that come with grief and loss.

In recent years, memorial services and funerals are often called celebrations of life. I feel that this is a healthy change and more accurately describes the essence of the gathering. I also believe that leaning into your grief means finding ways to celebrate the life of your loved one far beyond the time when a formal service is over. In the Jewish custom of Shiva, families gather for seven days in the home of the deceased to mourn and to share stories of their loved ones. Telling stories is a beautiful way to celebrate the lives of those we have lost. I love services where people are encouraged to spontaneously share their memories of the deceased. There is inevitably at least one story that causes those who are gathered to erupt into laughter. These stories celebrate the life that has been snuffed out yet lives on in the memories we hold dear. The Hispanic culture also has a special time for celebrating the lives of lost loved ones called Dia de los Muertos or Day of the Dead. Typically observed on the days before and after All Saints Day, this is a time for the extended family and friends of the deceased to gather in joyful celebration of those who have died during the past year, particularly through sharing memories.

Sharing stories doesn't need to be limited to special days and times or occur in places of worship. Sometimes, just going through old pictures with friends and reminiscing can help ease the pain of grief. The gospels tell of the disciples gathering to share memories of Jesus, process his death and wonder about the return he promised. It was the stories the disciples told as they shared the good news of his resurrection that became the source of our gospels. Never underestimate the power of story to help us heal.

In addition to religious and cultural rituals, there are many personal means by which to honor the life of someone close to us. A man who had been instrumental in an urban revitalization project was honored by former co-workers and his wife with the placement of a memorial marker at one corner of the property that had been brought back to life. Similarly, making donations to a meaningful charity in the name of the deceased is another way of honoring their life. One of the things we did after my father-in-law died was take a peace lily to the senior living apartment building where he had been living and placed it in their main gathering area for the people there to remember him by. Another woman, whose wife was pregnant with their first child, recorded her dying mother reading a book to the unborn baby. As the child grew, she was able to look at the book and listen to her grandmother reading it to her. They also placed photos of both her deceased grandparents on the refrigerator door, so their daughter always knew who these important people were in her life.

During COVID, so many deaths occurred without benefit of a funeral or memorial of any kind, which was a deep loss in and of itself. One woman whose mother passed away during the early days of COVID invited friends and relatives to write and send memories of her mother with the intention of creating a scrapbook of their stories. This was a wonderful way of celebrating her mother's life and remembering what a caring, supportive, and generous woman her mother had been and how many peoples' lives she had touched.

Another ritual that celebrates the life of a loved one is through the scattering of ashes. This can provide closure for those left behind and give them a gentle memory to hold onto. Often ashes are scattered in places that held special meaning for the deceased. Beau, whose wife died of brain cancer, spread her ashes in multiple places that had been special to her or that she had dreamed of seeing but never had the chance—a beach in Hawaii, Stonehenge, Grand Coulee dam, which had been a favorite spot to visit, and the ball parks they had dreamed of visiting together. Visits to these kinds of special places can bring a sense of connection, presence, and peace. The following is a poem I wrote following the scattering of my own mother's ashes.

The Scattering

A sparkling day,
sun-glitter on water,
the way it so seldom is
except in our memory.
I hold you in my hands,
blood and bone reduced
to dust,
as ordained from the beginning.
And then I release you.
As the wind takes you,
playfully creating scallops on the sand,
your joy rises,

your homecoming complete
at the place where
sea and shore embrace,
the mystical union
between human and divine.
I watch you cross over,
even while a trace of you remains,
a film on my fingers
and the sparkling shimmer of a tear.
The wind picks up,
carrying music on its wings.
Let the dancing begin.

One of the things we automatically do when we are grieving is to remember, even though our memories often lead to pain. Nonetheless, remembering is part of the journey of grief. Our memories are how our loved ones stay with us, and we treasure those memories as the sweetness that remains, continuing to bless us long after they are gone. Michelle O'Rourke, in a book about Henri Nouwen's spirituality of dying, states, "We remember them, not because they left us, but because they changed us."[17] Remembering honors our loved ones and the ways in which they impacted our lives, the blessings we received by the simple fact of their existence.

Photographs are a wonderful catalyst for retrieving memories, inciting laughter, tears, and long walks down memory lane. Treasured objects also touch us in ways that photos or words often cannot. My mother taught me to

---

[17] O'Rourke, *Befriending Death: Henri Nouwen and a Spirituality of Dying,* p. 60

embroider as a kid, and she herself embroidered numerous dish towels, handkerchiefs, and other decorative items. In order to keep her embroidery thread separated by color, she placed them in between the pages of an old Readers Digest. This magazine, bulging with a rainbow of thread, was an image of my childhood that was embedded in my memory. After she died, my sister and I were helping my dad go through some of Mom's things in preparation for his move to an assisted living facility. It was tedious work, and I was grumbling about how much junk had been collected over the years as I opened yet another box. Removing some old newspapers from the top, what should I see, but that worn Readers Digest and its multi-colored contents. I picked it up and immediately burst into tears. This tangible memento of times spent embroidering with my mother was so bittersweet, and despite the tears, I was grateful for the memories it engendered and for my mother who gave me so much.

Often, people hold onto items that had special meaning to the deceased. My mother-in-law collected angels, so we made sure that each granddaughter got to choose one of those angels to remember her by. My husband wears my dad's ski jacket in the winter and is reminded of his vitality and love of skiing. A young woman aged sixteen was brought to my therapy office by her father. She had lost her mother in a tragic boating accident that the girl witnessed firsthand. Kyla's trauma, grief, and loss were overwhelming, and the one she would normally go to for comfort and reassurance was gone. I asked her how her mother used to comfort her, and she described lying in bed next to her mom and holding her hand.

Seeking to give her something tangible to replicate that experience, I was able to find a small white stone figurine of cupped hands that was the perfect size for Kyla to cradle her thumb inside. This object became a steady source of soothing memories and comfort that sustained her through the most difficult times of grieving. Any tangible reminder you have of your lost loved one can be a way in which to remember, to receive comfort, and to heal.

Holding on to some of these mementos that have special meaning is an important part of the grief process. Being able to see or hold these items can stir fond memories, remind us of special times, speak to us of the person's identity and character. Whether it is jewelry, artwork, treasured possessions, clothing, an old letter, or collectibles, these items can give us comfort and help us stay connected to the person who is gone from our presence but not from our memory.

In the midst of this time of leaning into grief, it is easy to forget to take care of yourself. You may still be trying to do all the things that life demands—go to work, do household chores, fulfill family responsibilities, and cope with the practical tasks of death, and it is easy for your personal needs to drop to the bottom of the list. Nonetheless, you still need to eat healthy foods, exercise, and get plenty of sleep. You might even pamper yourself a little with a nice, hot bubble bath, a spa day, or time outdoors.

However, sometimes self-care is not enough. At some point you may become aware that you need more help than a bubble bath or brisk walk can fix. If you feel that you are descending into depression, feeling spiritually adrift or unable to function, it's probably time to seek help. Let your friends know you're struggling. Often, when the loss is fresh, friends will rally around without needing to be reminded. But when the loss is not theirs and normal life resumes, sometimes people forget that you are still grieving, still struggling. It's okay to let them know that for you the grief isn't over. Ask them to come over and keep you company when you're having a rough day. Invite them to go for a walk with you or go on a scenic drive to a place that soothes your soul. Or stay home and look at old photos, tell stories, laugh and cry together. Exchange lots of hugs. And silence is okay too. Sometimes just having someone to sit in silence with is a great comfort—no need to say anything, no need to "keep it together," just sitting with a friend who can hold your grief with you for a while.

> *Healing begins when we find the courage to take our pain out of its isolation and bring it into the open. When we name it and share it, not only is it easier to bear, but we come to realize that we suffer in communion with all of humanity.*[18]

Sometimes it might be enough to read a book like this one, that honors where you are and gives you comfort and hope. You can find a list of other resources in the appendices. It's also possible that you need professional

[18] O'Rourke, *Befriending Death: Henri Nouwen and a Spirituality of Dying,* p.74

help from a therapist, pastor, or spiritual director. Many people are helped by joining a grief group, finding that sharing their story with others who can relate is both comforting and a source of growth and hope. We are a culture that values a do-it-yourself mindset, and admitting that you need help is often difficult to do. Yet the stigma that once surrounded seeking professional help is waning, in part because so many people, especially in the wake of COVID, are seeking counseling themselves. It's important to realize that asking for help is not a sign of weakness, but an acknowledgement that some things are just too hard to bear alone.

Debby's Story

A middle-aged mother of an adult son, Debby received a phone call one hot August day to tell her that her adult son had been hit by a car on the side of a freeway offramp and was in critical condition. For two weeks, Debby was at his bedside for one procedure after another, wavering between hope and despair, as her son improved one day and took a step back the next. There wasn't one system of his body that hadn't been impacted by this horrific accident, and sadly, doctors took him off the respirator exactly two weeks after the accident.

Debby was like a zombie in the following weeks, performing the necessary tasks of death on autopilot. Yet every time she laid down to rest, traumatic images of her son's broken body and the multitude of medical interventions he endured would render sleep impossible. She cried for weeks on end. The first three months were like a tsunami, during which she prayed to die. But even in her darkest moments, she knew that her son would want her to live. "I choose life," became her personal mantra. For her, this meant leaning into her grief as much as possible.

Debby journaled daily, pouring her feelings onto the page in order to get a measure of relief from the emotional onslaught. She went through a grief recovery program twice. She sought out a counselor, attended Adult Children of Alcoholics meetings, and talked with friends and family members. As part of her ordination process for ministry, she participated in a program of clinical pastoral education, which includes hands on training in chaplaincy work. Through all of these experiences, Debby was giving herself permission to feel her pain and let it heal her. While the worst of her grief eased after about three months, the entire process of her healing lasted for over two years.

Believe it or not, eventually there will come a time when you feel a nudge to begin re-engaging with life. This will likely come with feelings of ambivalence. Your home may have become a cocoon of sorts, a safe place for you to grieve and heal. You may feel leery about re-entering the outside world, and that's perfectly understandable.

Despite this hesitancy, you will begin to see re-entering the world as possible, and you will take baby steps in that direction. You might discover that you feel the urge to resume a former hobby, attend social gatherings again, spend time with friends, return to your previous church activities, or take up new pursuits that are life-giving. You will feel the stirring of energy again. You will be surprised to find yourself laughing or humming under your breath. This doesn't mean that your grief is over, but it has changed. It has been integrated into your life story, one part of who you are instead of being the *whole* story. Grief no longer defines you, but it has changed you in sometimes indefinable ways. It likely will have made you more compassionate, more attuned to the suffering of others. You have sat on the razor's edge between life and death, and you have chosen life.

> *"I know*
> *there are days*
> *when the only thing*
> *more brave than leaving*
> *this house*
> *is coming back to it."*
> —Jan Richardson[19]

Spiritual Practice

"It came home to me that the most profound blessings we will ever know are those that meet us in the place of our deepest loss and inspire us to choose to live again." Take some time to consider these words from Jan Richardson.[20] If you wish, journal about the blessings that have come in the midst of your grief and what has inspired you to choose life in all its messiness, pain, joy, uncertainty, and blessing.

---

[19] Richardson, *The Cure for Sorrow: A Book of Blessings for Times of Grief,* 39

[20] Richardson, *Circle of Grace: A Book of Blessings for the Seasons,* p. xiii

Prayer

Holy One, thank you for the gift of the people in our lives, the ones who are still living, and the ones who are gone from our midst. Walk with us on this journey of grief. Lend us your shoulder as we shed our tears, hear our groaning, and remind us that while mourning lasts through the long dark nights, joy will come with the morning light. Stir our memories, our gratitude, our desire to honor our saints in this world and the next. Give us strength for the journey of grief, and may we always know your loving presence beside us along the way. Amen.

Interlude

Tsunami

A tsunami of grief
washes over me—
wave after wave
of pain and loss.
The waters have gathered,
building up beyond the horizon,
collecting the impact
of too many losses
until they cannot
be contained any longer.
Denial cannot hold them back,
cannot pretend it's fine—
I'm fine.
I'm not.
It's too much.
And so I dive
into the flood,
acquiesce to the currents
of grief,
accept that I am not
strong enough,
ride the waves
until grace washes me up
on the shores of love,
my fingers gripping the sand.

Chapter 6

Can Faith Survive?

'Some nights in the midst of this
loneliness I swing among the scattered stars
at the end of the thin thread of faith alone."[21]
—Wendell Berry

When cruel death casts its shadow over your life, when your pain is too much to bear, it is not unusual to be angry at God, to feel abandoned by God or worse, that God just doesn't care. Some might even wonder, as they try to answer the existential "Why" question, if God exists at all. In times of profound loss, all of these thoughts and feelings are perfectly understandable and even to be expected. Anger at God isn't going to cause a bolt of lightning to strike you from heaven. God is more understanding than that. God knows your grief and our human need to have someone to blame. God understands grief intimately through the loss of his son on Calvary's hill, having watched him die an agonizing death on the cross. The darkened skies of Good Friday and the shuddering of an earthquake are eloquent portrayals of God's grief and ours. Through Jesus, God is profoundly aware of the human

[21] Berry, *Jayber Crow: A Novel*

condition, and Her divine compassion is as vast as the stars and as intimate as an embrace.

Joan's Story

Joan was a pastor and seminary professor when she first met Carly in one of her classes. Carly was in an abusive relationship and sometimes came to Joan for advice. After Carly graduated from seminary, the two women, both pastors in the same denomination, became friends, enjoying an occasional movie or dinner out. Over time, their friendship became something more, and eventually, they married. Coming from an abusive background herself, Joan felt that Carly was the only person she had ever felt safe with, her true home. The depth of their love for each other was beyond anything they had ever experienced.

One day, about three years after their marriage, Carly was wiping up a spill from the kitchen floor when she felt a strange sensation in her arm. Within days, she began having episodes of aphasia, an inability to form words. When they went to the doctor, he immediately referred them to a neurosurgeon who ordered an MRI and various other tests. He found that Carly had a massive and rare brain tumor. After seven hours of surgery, the surgeon could only remove half of it. To excise the entire mass would have killed her. At that point, Joan became Carly's caregiver, moving a hospital bed into their living room. For a full year, she cared for her beloved wife while still pastoring a church. Watching Carly's decline was torture. The aphasia worsened, and they had to develop a special language for everyday foods that Carly could eat. Bananas became "long yellow," and Cheetos were "orange crunchy." At times, Carly would become combative, a side effect of the massive amount of steroids she was being given, fighting against medications and the necessary physical care that her condition demanded. Through it all, Joan prayed relentlessly, making deals with God, begging that her beloved not be taken from her. The prayers were to no avail, and Carly passed away one year after her diagnosis.

Joan's grief was an abyss of darkness, and sadly, her faith died along with her wife. All her prayers had gone unanswered, had been for nothing. She was still pastoring a church at the time and felt like a hypocrite every time she stood in the pulpit. Once she retired, she stopped attending church altogether. She doesn't pray anymore, doesn't believe that God answers prayer. However, she does continue to follow Jesus' teachings and lives her life with love as her guiding principle.

Joan is not alone in her rejection of a God who is often portrayed as one who answers our every prayer. The woman whose mother died during COVID also felt that her prayers had gone unanswered. Despite her work as a hospital chaplain, her view of God has changed dramatically. She no longer believes that God is intimately involved in the daily events of our lives, saying, "I don't think God tinkers very much." Nonetheless, she does occasionally have a sense of divine presence that gives her peace. Eileen, whose son died of liver failure in his thirties, also felt angry with God even though she continued to attend church. She alternated between feeling disconnected from God and randomly sensing the divine Presence hovering near her.

I am struck by the disparity of people's spiritual responses to loss. From Joan's rejection of God to Heather's doubts to Susan's spiritual healing and transformation (see Chapter Two) and the many who felt that their faith was strengthened and gave them comfort in their grief, there is a wide spectrum of how loss impacts faith. The important thing to remember is that none of these responses is wrong. Belief is highly personal, and faith fluctuates as we move through the experiences of life, both the good and the bad. The following quote from Eugene Peterson speaks to the idea that even atheism can be considered a spiritual response to suffering:

> Atheists can be among a Christian's best friends. Atheists, for instance, whose atheism develops out of protest: angry about what is wrong with the world, are roused to passionate defiance. That a good God permits the birth of crippled children, that a loving God allows rape and torture, that a sovereign God stands aside while the murderous regime of a Genghis Khan or an Adolf Hitler runs its course—such outrageous paradoxes simply cannot be countenanced. So God is eliminated. The removal of God does not reduce the suffering, but it does wipe out the paradox. Such atheism is not the result of logical (or illogical) thought; it is sheer protest. Anger

> over the suffering and unfairness in the world becomes anger against the God who permits it. Defiance is expressed by denial. Such atheism is commonly full of compassion. It suffers and rages. It is deeply spiritual, in touch with the human condition and eternal values.[22]

People who have lost a special someone too soon are *angry!* We raise our fists at God and rail about the unfairness of this world where it sometimes seems that, as Billy Joel would put it, "only the good die young!" We want answers, and there are none. We live in a random world, and contrary to popular opinion, not everything happens for a reason. People of faith are not exempt from tragedy. Cancer doesn't discriminate. Viruses like COVID-19 afflict us all in one way or another. Fatal accidents happen without regard for a person's faith or goodness of character.

Jesus addresses this issue directly when questioned about the blind man whose sight he restored in John 9. People in the crowd asked who had sinned, the man or his parents. Jesus denied that the blindness had anything to do with sin. And in Matthew 5:45 (NRSV), Jesus declares, "(God) makes his sun rise on the evil and on the good and sends rain on the righteous and on the unrighteous." In other words, calamity and tragedy can strike us all in this flawed world we call home. The reality is that God is not

---

[22] Peterson, cited in *A Guide to Prayer for All God's People, p. 322,* Ruben & Job, eds.

the author of suffering, but balm for the souls of those who suffer.

When my father-in-law was in the Air Force decades ago, he was stationed at a radar installation at the far end of the Aleutian chain, only miles away from the coast of Russia. When he first arrived on this remote and barren island, he noticed that all the sidewalks had waist-high sturdy rope strung along the pathways. He wondered what the rope was for, but anyone he asked would just reply, "You'll see." The next morning, he emerged from the bunk house to encounter gale force winds that nearly blew him off his feet. Almost instinctively, he grabbed for the rope next to the walkway. The thick rope allowed him to get to the radar building without being blown off the island and into the sea.

For some reason, this story stuck with me until I came to realize that it might have a deeper meaning than a factoid about the powerful winds of the Bering Sea. Most of us have been through some severe storms in our lives, both literal and metaphorical. The problem is that many of us believe that God sent the storm or even that God IS the storm. But I think the storm is just life, this world we live in, in both its grandeur and fury, and God is the rope. God is who we hang onto when the winds of life are blowing stronger than we can manage on our own. We are not given to know when those storms will come or why or who was to blame, but we do know that God will be our rope, our hope, and our comforter.

Another thing we can know is that Jesus' death on the cross was a message of solidarity with all human suffering. Because of the cross, Jesus knows what it is to suffer; God knows what it is to lose a beloved Son. When we weep, God weeps.

> "Christianity is the only world religion that confesses a God who suffers. It is not that popular an idea, even among Christians. We prefer a God who prevents suffering, only that is not the God we have got. What the cross teaches us is that God's power is not the power to force human choices and end human pain. It is, instead, the power to pick up the shattered pieces and make something holy out of them—not from a distance, but right close up." —Barbara Brown Taylor[23]

If your heart is broken, you'll find God right there; if you're kicked in the gut, he'll help you catch your breath." Psalm 34:18 (MSG)

Nonetheless, it is hard to know how to pray when you are doubting God's existence or are carrying such anger for a divine being who failed to protect, heal, or save your loved one. In the book, *Prayers in the Night,* author Tish Harrison Warren, an Anglican priest, shares her own spiritual struggle. She had lost her father unexpectedly, then suffered two miscarriages over the course of the next seven months. During those long months of darkness, she says, "I was a priest who couldn't pray. I didn't know how

---

[23] Taylor, *God in Pain*

to approach God anymore. There were too many things to say, too many questions without answers. My depth of pain overshadowed my ability with words. And, more painfully, I couldn't pray because I wasn't sure how to trust God."[24]

I'm sure many of us can identify with these words. When we are hurt, angry, and suffering, when we struggle to understand how a loving God could allow our loved ones to be taken from us, it is hard to find words that feel remotely acceptable to God or others. Yet, a trip through the Psalms is proof enough that there is nothing we can't say to God. God is big enough to receive our fury, resentment, and anguish, and love us anyway. Truthfully, we don't need words at all. A friend who suffers from occasional episodes of depression once said to me, "Let your pain be your prayer." Your tears, your wailing, your roars of anger will not go unheard. Madeline L'Engle is quoted as saying, "It is when things go wrong, when the good things do not happen, when our prayers seem to have been lost, that God is most present. We do not need the sheltering wings when things go smoothly. We are closest to God in the darkness, stumbling along blindly."[25]

Spiritual Practice

Read the following poem. Meditate on this theme that to love means to also be hurt by the loss of a relationship through estrangement, divorce, or death. Have you been angry at God or drifted away from organized religion when comfort and answers eluded you? Journal your thoughts and feelings.

---

[24] Warren, *Prayer in the Night,* pg. 12

[25] L'Engle, cited in *A Rhythm of Prayer,* p. 62

Has anyone been
untouched by grief,
not known the sting of loss,
the agony of life's endings?
Has anyone
not cursed at God
for the sorrows
of this world?
Have we not wondered,
"Why?"
Yet death visits us all,
waits on our door step
for the axe to fall,
poised to swoop in
to steal our treasure,
leave us bereft.
And yet,
we dare to love,
to risk the cost,
for without love,
we are nothing.

Prayer

Where are you, God? Why does it feel like when we are hurting the most, when we need answers, you seem to be absent? We are lost, angry, confused, adrift. We need something, some<u>one</u> to hold onto, but it's so hard to find you in the darkness that surrounds us. Please help us to see you. Help us to feel your Presence, your loving arms enfolding us. Receive our tears, our shouts, our curses, our pain. Hold us next to your heart until we can open our eyes, can breathe again, can lift our heads, begin to see light dawning. Never let us go. Amen.

Interlude

Trust

It seems that when
the worst things have happened,
have proved to you
that control is an illusion,
stress leaves you.
You let go,
leave things in God's hands
and walk step by step,
just doing the next thing.
This surrender
allows you to breathe
and then to trust
in the words of a saint,
"All shall be well."
Not easy, not an end
to troubles,
but a certainty
that God is with us,
and goodness will come
in its time.

Chapter Seven

Holy Moments

"Where there is sorrow, there is holy ground."[26]
—Oscar Wilde

Woven in and out of the stories of people who have experienced deep loss are unexplainable moments of comfort, peace, presence, dreams, coincidences, and even joy. Some would say these events are mystical messages from God or from our lost loved ones, some would dismiss them as mere coincidence, but for many, they are a source of comfort and reassurance. Following is my own experience of the day my father died, written many weeks after it happened:

My dad died. This shouldn't have come as a shock. After all, he was 96 years old. But he believed so adamantly in his own indestructibility that I think we had unconsciously begun to believe it, too. He died, and I wasn't there. I wanted to be there. I had expected to be there, but instead it was my husband who held his work-worn hands, prayed over him, and attended his gentle

[26] As cited in *The Wild Edge of Sorrow,* Weller, p. 8

crossing from this life to the next. My crafty father, who always hated to see me cry, had found a way to make his exit without waterworks.

I had been leading a retreat many miles away when I got the call. A young camp leader had to break the news, "Your father may not make it through the day." When I spoke to my husband, he told me, "Even if you leave right now, you won't get here in time." So, I stayed long enough to wrap up the retreat before heading home across a mountain pass.

My keening cries reverberated around the car as it became a container for the deepening whirlpool of my grief. One is never ready for that brutal blow of loss, even when it is past time, when life has been seeping away over many months and they are ready to go, when death is a welcome release. I grieved for this man who had been so difficult to love in life, so hard to please, so maddeningly obstinate. And yet, here I was, swamped by the intensity of my loss.

I did not go straight home to the arms of my husband, but drove instead to the nursing home where my father's body still lay, peacefully waiting. Nurses greeted me with hugs and tears and stories of his last few days. "How does it end," he'd asked, and when the nurse, knowing not to assume he meant life, questioned how *what* ended, he had responded, "The prayer." Then, armed with her answer, he had begun to pray. As aides helped him into his pajamas, brushed his teeth and put him to bed, he prayed on. Finally, reaching the end of his plea to the God of life and death, he issued an emphatic "Amen."

Touched by this story and grateful to the one who told it, I made the long walk down the hall, steeling myself for what I would see. Taking a deep breath at the door, I peered into his room—and nearly laughed.

Mouth agape in characteristic fashion, he looked as though he had just fallen asleep in front of the TV and would awaken at any moment to resume reading the paper without skipping a beat. It was a scene played out so many times, it had become a family joke. But this time, there was no TV, no newspaper. My eyes drank him in, noticing every detail—pale drawn skin, sunken cheeks, his huge hands now cold and still. I had been watching him breathe for weeks, and even now I waited for the rise and fall of his chest. I even imagined I saw it, so strong was his physical presence and my own longing, until I realized that an open window was stirring the air and ruffling his hospital gown.

I spoke to him. I touched his hands and rubbed his feet one last time, unwilling to stop loving him in the way that had become so precious these past weeks. It seemed to me that his vulnerability had allowed him to receive these gestures of a love I had never before been able to express. It felt like Jesus washing the feet of his disciples. My father had always been a stoic, inept in the giving and receiving of love, yet always hungry for admiration and a sense of belonging. Not given to emotional expression, he had not told me "I love you" until I was an adult and out of the house. But his diminishing health had changed all that. His failing body and his helplessness somehow unlocked something inside him, and he was able to communicate a love and gratitude that healed old wounds in me and opened up a wellspring of answering love. His eyes would light up when I walked in the room, and his facial expressions, so familiar to me, told me everything I needed to know. It was as though the more his body failed, the more his heart opened.

And now he was gone, entered into glory, into the place of ultimate belonging, ultimate healing. But I could also feel his spirit lingering to say good-bye, to make sure I was okay. And despite the sharp pain of loss, I was. All of life is a prayer, it seems to me, and it ends with a resounding "Amen."

As I drove home that afternoon, my son called me to see how I was doing. He and his girlfriend had been hiking in the red rocks of Colorado when they got the word. It was a place my father would have loved, and they had continued to explore as they reminisced about him and his love of the great outdoors. Later, as they drove home, my son said, "Grandpa is probably dancing with Grandma in heaven right now." As soon as the words were out of his mouth, they saw a sign on the side of the street—Patsy's Ice Cream Shop. My mother's name was Patsy. And as if I needed further confirmation that all was well in heaven and on earth, when I finally drove up the country road to our home, a perfect rainbow arced over the valley.

My husband has his own story to tell about a mystical moment following the death of his father. At age 90, Jean had been suffering from a failing heart valve and needed to have it replaced. The snag was that he had lost a kidney due to cancer two years prior, and the surgery would put a great deal of stress on the remaining kidney. There were some tests that needed to be done to ensure that he was a good candidate for the procedure, and those tests would need to be done with contrast, which is particularly hard on kidneys. An extreme reaction to one of the tests put him in the ICU and then the cardiovascular unit. He was starting to rebound despite a case of pneumonia, so they let him come home with us. After four days of ups and downs, we finally took him back to the hospital when he became delirious. His lungs were full of fluid, and the Lasix used to treat him also strains the kidneys. Nonetheless, he improved to the point where the heart doctors felt they could proceed with the valve replacement in two days' time. Meanwhile, the ER docs decided to draw more of the fluid off his lungs through a tube in his chest rather than stressing his kidney with more Lasix. It was in the midst of this procedure that Jean's heart stopped. After over thirty minutes of chest compressions without signs of life, the doctors ceased their efforts. My father-in-law was gone.

The next morning, after many tears and little sleep, my husband woke early and decided that he might as well get up and get on with all of the overwhelming tasks ahead of him. He swung his legs over the side of the bed and glanced at his alarm clock. It read 5:19 AM. His father's birthday is May 19th. Suddenly Tom knew that his dad was looking down from heaven and sending a message that he was okay and reunited with his beloved wife who had died two years before. Tom went on with his day, beginning the arduous task of making decisions and arrangements, searching for important documents, and starting the process of emptying out his dad's apartment. When he emerged from his office to show me the safety deposit key he had finally found, he asked me what was for dinner. "I don't even know what time it is," he said and turned to look at the kitchen clock. It read 5:19 PM. Even the most skeptical person would have a hard time labeling this as a coincidence!

Many people who have been present when a loved one's spirit left their body have described an indefinable sense of presence, an opening of the translucent veil between earth and heaven. Spiritual teachers often call this the thin place or liminal space, when we are standing on the boundary of opposites, where we know without question that both realities are true. These are precious moments of transition, when we are present at the end of the life of a loved one, and we are standing on the boundary between life and death. This is holy ground.

Heather experienced this at the moment of her mother's death and has experienced it many times since in her work as a hospital chaplain. Sharon, whose story is described in Chapter One, felt it when a flock of geese passed by the window at the moment of her father's death. At one point during the death vigil for her adult son, Eileen was standing at his bedside when she suddenly felt surrounded by sunshine and light. She said it was as though, "someone was holding me up." Ann, whose alcoholic and mentally ill mother died of sepsis after a fall, had a vision shortly afterward of a gathering of women in a meadow where Jesus was present. In this vision, her mother was there, sitting with the other women in a circle and being anointed a priestess. Despite her emotional challenges, Ann's mother had been very spiritual and had dreamed of becoming an Episcopal priest, so this dream seemed to be a message of fulfillment and peace for Ann as she grieved. Jen, who spent weeks helping her mom care for her cancer-ridden father prior to his death, knows his spirit is near whenever she notices that the pictures on her walls are crooked. Her dad abhorred symmetry, so in life he was constantly tipping pictures off kilter. Now, the crooked pictures make her smile. But she always straightens them again.

Heidi, whose husband died after years of ill health, was on a flight to attend her niece's college graduation when she had the sensation of being in a warm bubble and absolutely knew that it was the presence of her late husband. Later, she and some of the girls who were graduating went shopping at a quaint hardware store in the town where the graduation was to be held. They discovered that one wall held a display of moose wall hangings, stuffed animals, ornaments, and other moose trinkets. Heidi's husband's favorite animal was the moose. The girls with Heidi were convinced that Steve's presence was with them, so they bought a stuffed moose and took it to the graduation ceremony. Uncle Steve got to see his niece's graduation after all.

Chris' Story

After several attempts at in vitro fertilization, Chris' son and his wife were finally successful and looked forward with great anticipation to the birth of a son or daughter. However, they discovered early in the pregnancy that the child had a heart defect. Chris' daughter-in-law is a nurse, and she felt that, though difficult, she would be able to cope with that. They made the decision to move forward with the pregnancy. However, when the baby, a beautiful little boy, was born several weeks early, it was discovered that he had multiple other birth defects, including the absence of an anus. The heart issues were also worse than expected. The child would have faced life with a feeding tube, colostomy, and several heart surgeries as he grew. The doctors repeatedly reassured the parents that these issues were fixable, and the family consented to the several surgeries that followed. For a while, it appeared that baby Lincoln was responding to treatments and holding his own, but eventually the impact of so much trauma to his body was too much. He passed away in his mother's arms with the entire family surrounding him. He was twelve days old.

The family was devastated. As Chris reflected on what had happened, she was struck by how outwardly perfect the baby's body had been at birth and how violated it eventually was by the procedures he endured. "They cut him to pieces," she said in the aftermath. This agony for his suffering was nearly unbearable for her. It was all she could think about in the days and weeks following his death. She wondered if they had been so selfish in their desire to keep him alive that they had been partially responsible for her grandson's suffering. Day by day, it seemed her grief got worse instead of better.

Then, one day as Chris was out running errands, mind continuing to ruminate on Lincoln's death, she actually *felt* him get into the car with her. She saw him as a young man, grown and healthy, sitting in the passenger seat of her car. And then he spoke to her. "Grandma, you've got to stop it. I'm not in pain anymore." Immediately, her anguish lifted. She said that Lincoln's appearance solidified everything she believes about God, heaven, and the afterlife. Tears streamed down her face. As she related this story to me, she said, "This was as real to me as anything I've ever experienced in my life." Lincoln appeared to her one more time, as she was praying in the temple a few days later, saying, "I love you, Grandma, more than you know."

> *"There is some strange intimacy between grief and aliveness, some sacred exchange between what seems unbearable and what is most exquisitely alive."* [27]

It's important to note that this kind of mystical experience doesn't happen to everyone. If you haven't received such a gift, it doesn't mean there is something wrong with you or with the manner in which you are grieving. Grief is different for everyone. Or maybe you have had such an experience but didn't consider it to be sacred per se. Many holy moments are more prosaic, but equally moving and comforting. Our lost loved ones often show up in our dreams, especially early on in our grieving. I once dreamt that I was waiting in a line at the movie theater, and my long-dead mother came up behind me and tapped me on the shoulder. I asked her where she had been, that we had been looking for her everywhere. I still remember how glad I was to see her. When I awoke, I was incredibly grateful for that gift of an experience with her, even if only in a dream.

---

[27] Weller, *Wild Edge,* p.1

Sometimes the holy moments occur *before* death. They might be as simple as singing familiar songs with your loved one as their body edges ever closer to the veil between life and death and being grateful for the love and joy of family. It can be watching cheesy television shows and laughing hysterically at how bad they are. Any activity that knits you together with laughter, music, and love can be holy.

It can also be a moment of clarity in which your mind looks on from a distance at the same time as you are engaging lovingly with a dying friend or family member. For example, when my mother was in a nursing home with dementia, my dad and I took her a piece of huckleberry pie for her birthday. The care facility had placed a little goody bag on her bedside table. I opened it and found, among other small items, a bottle of soap bubbles, so I got them out and blew bubbles for my mom. Even as her mind was wasting away, there was enough body memory left that she knew the bubbles were for popping, and she batted at them for several minutes, squealing and laughing like a kid at play. This too was a holy moment. It was a beautiful gift in the midst of my ongoing grief as I watched her fade away.

Spiritual Practice

Look back at your memories of the dying or death of a loved one and pay attention to those moments when there was joy despite the pain, laughter in the midst of tears, a sense of the holy imbuing a special moment when the world stood still and shone with a heavenly light. Breathe into those moments and memories, let them fill you with comfort. Be aware of your loved one's continued presence in your life. Watch for signs of coincidences that might be messages from the beyond. You might want to write them down, draw a picture that reminds you of that moment, or look for pictures that are reminiscent of that time. Cherish your dreams. If there is an object of yours or your loved one that played a part in your holy moment, place it in a location where you will see it often and remember.

Prayer

Holy Mystery, open our eyes to the experiences that are beyond our comprehension. Help us to receive these moments as gifts of love that connect all that has gone before, all that is, and all that will be. Let these moments bring us comfort, assure us of the continuance of Life beyond life, and bind us to our loved ones with a love that transcends our earthly lives and lives forever in your infinite heart. Amen.

Interlude

Miracles

What do miracles look like?
Rainbows in a pure blue sky,
or streams of light
emanating
from foreboding storm clouds.
What wonder is to be found
at the intersection
between life and death,
sorrow and joy,
loss and gift?
How do we respond
to the moments
that leave us breathless,
that defy belief
and cause us to believe
at the same time?
Receive, beloved.
simply receive.

Chapter Eight

Comfort

Blessed are those who mourn, for they shall be comforted.
Matthew 5:4 (NIV)

After my mother died, I felt like I had lost my center. For years, I had lost her to her dementia, lost my identity as a daughter as we arranged for her care, communicated with her residential facility, checked in with my dad regularly for reports on how she was doing and visited when I could. Now that she was truly gone and I was no longer a long-distance caregiver of sorts, I was suddenly free to just be her daughter again. And that opened up a deep canyon of grief that left me feeling adrift. One day, I decided to visit our church's prayer garden in hopes of finding some peace. I walked the small labyrinth and sat on a bench in the center where I let go of my need to be strong and allowed the tears to flow. As my eyes took in the stark desert landscape, I began to sense a presence so tangible I could almost see it—a swirling, translucent female figure circling me and offering me comfort. In that moment, I knew this was the Holy Spirit that Jesus promised the disciples he would send before he was taken up into heaven. I sat there for a long time, feeling her holding me, reassuring me, whispering that all would be well. After several minutes, I found that I was able to breathe again, deep full breaths that filled me with a sense of peace and the knowledge that I was not alone.

I have long believed that the Holy Spirit is a feminine aspect of the Godhead. To imagine that a single gender could fully express the nature of the Divine seems preposterous to me, so it was not foreign for me to see the Holy Spirit in this way and receive the comfort of Her presence with me that day. I also believe that God can show up in whatever way we are most inclined to recognize Him or Her.

When Jesus spoke to his disciples about the One that would come after him, he was promising that the Holy Spirit would be with them, that they would not be orphaned, but would receive another manifestation of God that would never leave them without comfort. In John 14:16, Jesus refers to this holy presence as comforter, counselor, or helper, depending on the translation. This promise is something we can cling to when we are deep in the throes of our sorrow. Certainly, many people have shared experiences of someone who offered them comfort during times of deep grief, whether strangers, casual acquaintances, or close friends. Indeed, there are often angels in our midst.

Jen's Story

Jen's father was diagnosed with esophageal cancer at the age of 73. It was aggressive and painful, and the family was warned that it would be a horrific death. Jen flew home to be with her family and help care for him in the final weeks of his life. Hospice was taking care of his medical needs, but the family had to deal with his vomiting, bleeding, and their futile attempts to get him to eat anything at all. His pain was out of control, and the entire family experienced the trauma of that. Despite this, they tried to keep their spirits up, cooking dinner together, listening to seventies music, singing along loudly and off-key, cherishing the moments when the pain was less intense, and their dad could join in. One day, a church friend came by and sang to Jen's dad. As she listened, Jen felt a profound sense of gratitude and comfort. It was a moment of peace in the midst of their nightmare.

There are many ways that we can access comfort during the times when our grief feels raw and deep. The people who shared their stories with me talked about activities like reading old letters from their loved one, listening to music that is tied to memories, cooking some of their favorite foods, wearing a piece of their clothing, or recreating a particular scent that evokes their essence. Others found that sharing memories with family and friends who knew their loved one well or looking at old photo albums with them brought the person back to life if only for a moment.

Visiting places that were meaningful to both you and the deceased can be particularly poignant. Ann lost her best friend to cancer a few years ago. The woman who died had been the co-founder of a communal artist colony and retreat center focused on the relationship between art and faith. The two women were both weavers and participated in many of the activities that took place in a beautiful weaving room with soaring windows that framed the stately ponderosa pines that populated the center grounds. Whenever Ann went to the guild, she could feel her friend's presence all around her, in the looms, the colors of the thread, the trees, and the river that flowed nearby.

Whenever I am in the woods or near a lake or stream that I know my parents would have loved, I feel their presence and comfort. This is especially true on the lake where I grew up. The lake and its surrounding hills feel like a womb, the umbilical cord still binding me to my parents and the love they had for me and for God's creation.

Scriptures can also bring comfort to a hurting heart. You can find a list of some of them in the appendices at the back of this book, but one passage that always speaks to me is Isaiah 53:3-5:

> *He was despised and rejected by men, a man of sorrows, and familiar with suffering. Like one from whom men hide their faces he was despised, and we esteemed him not. Surely, he took up our infirmities and carried our sorrows, yet we considered him stricken by God, smitten by him and afflicted. But he was pierced for our transgressions, he was crushed for our iniquities; the punishment that brought us peace was upon him, and by his wounds we are healed.* (NIV)

My own personal interpretation of Jesus' death on the cross was not that he was a scapegoat being punished for our sins—that evokes a punitive and vengeful deity rather than the loving and compassionate God that is demonstrated throughout scripture. Instead, I believe that Jesus came to become the connection between God and humanity, his death on the cross an act of solidarity with all of human suffering. It is no accident that upon Jesus' death, the curtain in the temple was torn in two. That curtain was what guarded the Holy of Holies and separated God's people from the Divine Presence. Jesus' death, as both fully human and fully divine, bridged the final gap between God and humankind forever.

Therefore, when we are grieving, we can be assured that Jesus knows our suffering, that he is with us in our pain, and that he can offer a comfort that is grounded in his own human experience. To imagine being held by a weeping Christ whose hands and feet still bear the scars of the cross, whose compassion for us breaks his own heart can be profoundly comforting in times when the pain of loss is beyond words.

The old-time hymn "There is a Balm in Gilead." speaks to human sorrow and the longing for hope and healing. It refers to a passage in Jeremiah 8:21-9:1 in which Jeremiah grieves for the Israelites who have been exiled from their homeland by conquering armies. Gilead was a region east of the Jordan River that was known for its spices, medicinal herbs, and healing balms. This hymn reassures us that healing is possible, that hope may be found, and that comfort is ours when we turn to our God for relief from our suffering. The chorus promises consolation for our struggles: "There is a balm in Gilead to make the wounded whole; there is a balm in Gilead to heal the *grieving* soul."[28] (italics indicate my interpretation)

Belief in some sort of afterlife is often a significant comfort for those who grieve. This is not restricted to the heaven referred to in the Bible. There are many cultures that have alternative ideas about what happens after death. One of my clients came to me after a dear friend had passed away, and she was struggling with the idea of whether there is something beyond our life on earth. She was not a person of faith, so this made it more difficult. Then I remembered the African belief that after death, the spirits of loved ones enter into creation—the trees, grass, stones, et cetera. The spirit world and the natural world are inextricably linked. The song, *Breaths,* by the African American group, Sweet Honey in the Rock, suggests that we can hear the voices of our ancestors in the crackling fire, the rustling leaves, the rush of ocean waves. It reassures us that "those who have died have never, never left; the dead are not under the earth."[29] This concept resonated with my client and helped her discover her own way of staying connected to her deceased friend.

In fact, I found this concept helpful in my own grief over the loss of my mom. She had loved gardening and particularly purple flowers or shrubs. I decided that if her spirit was going to be contained by anything on this earth, it would be purple flowers. This gave me another way to feel connected to her. Whenever I saw a lavender bush or

[28] United Methodist Hymnal, #375

[29] "Breaths," Sweet Honey in the Rock, Barnwell's Notes Co., 1980

purple petunias or blooming sage, I would know that her spirit was near. A similar concept often suggested for helping children deal with their grief is to identify a star in the sky that is the sparkling of their lost loved one's spirit. Having something tangible to help us stay connected to those we have lost is tremendously comforting and healing.

In the ancient Mayan culture, birth and death were inextricably linked. Many of their ruins have circular holes carved above the entrance of what were believed to be places of worship. The hole represented a birth canal and was a symbol of both birth and death, suggesting that for them, death was merely a portal to another level of existence.

I also think it helps to view life as energy. Energy doesn't die, but it transforms. Just as energy passes through many different stages on its way to our homes, so life transforms from one state to another. While the human body may die, the spark of that person's life lives on in our memories, in the stories we tell, in the ways we honor them through our actions and beliefs, and in the lives of subsequent generations.

Nonetheless, for some Christians, heaven is a biblical promise to cling to in times of grief. In John 12:32, Jesus proclaims, "And I, when I am lifted up from the earth, will draw all people to myself." (NIV) All people. There are no conditions or tests. Saint Peter is not going to be waiting at the pearly gates to determine our worthiness. For Christians, this hope of heavenly glory for our loved ones and the promise that we will see them again in the afterlife is profoundly comforting.

Spiritual Practice

"I will turn their mourning into gladness; I will give them comfort and joy instead of sorrow." —Jeremiah 31: 13b (NIV)

The Bible is full of these promises that despite the pain and suffering of this life, there will be comfort, there will be joy, there will be dancing. No one is exempt from this cycle of life and death, pain and promise, darkness and light. Consider the losses you have experienced in your life, both large and small, and look past those losses to the times when your pain has been replaced by joy or there has been a resurrection of some kind. A friend of mine was grieving her daughter's marriage to a man who was emotionally abusive and controlling. This went on for a few years, and then one morning, as my friend was praying, she heard a voice in her head say, "Perhaps all is not lost." She had no idea what that meant, but she stored those words in her heart. About a year later, her daughter called to tell her that her marriage was ending. My friend recalled the message she had been given and was grateful for its fulfillment.

1) Write down any episodes you have experienced where you received comfort and joy after a loss.
2) If you are in the midst of a recent loss and are still grieving, claim one of the scriptures from the back of the book to cling to until your time of deepest grief is past.
3) If someone you know is grieving, reach out to them with words of comfort and care.

Prayer

It is always light somewhere,
always dark somewhere.
O Author of the universe,
when you set the sun and moon
in the sky,
you did not erase the darkness
but gave us the promise
that light is contained
within the dark,
that light is present
even in the blackest of nights.
Shine your light now
on your children
who are suffering,
whose world feels
like unending gloom.
May they feel your Presence
like a warm embrace.
In the midst of sorrow,
may they know the comfort
of friends,
the gratitude for memories,
the recognition of blessings.
Remind us
that the light of loves lost
remains forever
in our hearts
and cannot be
blotted out. Amen.

Interlude

Hope

Walk courageously into the dark
carrying light.
Pray unceasingly,
that you be reminded
of Divine presence
in every moment.
Keep watch for signs of hope,
for they are easy to miss
among the voices of doom.
Take time to rest,
for weariness amplifies
dark imaginings.
Remember that in all things
one season gives way to another.
Dawn comes.
Walk on.

Chapter Nine

A Little Help From My Friends

A friend loves at all times, and a brother is born for adversity.
—Proverbs 17:17 (NIV)

As I shared in Chapter 7, when my father died, I was in the middle of leading a women's retreat an hour away from his nursing home. When I shared the news with these wonderful ladies, they quickly helped me revise the retreat schedule so I could leave as soon as possible. They helped pack up my belongings and hauled them out to my car. When I was ready to leave, they gathered around me and laid hands on me, praying for safe travels and for God's comforting presence in the days of grief ahead. It was a profound moment and one I will never forget.

One of the most common threads throughout the stories I've heard about grief is the importance of friends who supported those who grieve in ways both large and small. Friends prayed, brought meals, ran errands, provided a shoulder to cry on, cleaned, and answered phone calls—shielding grieving spouses, mothers, fathers, sons, and daughters from the curious and intrusive people who have the best of intentions but can sometimes be overwhelming. From picking up kids from school to actually moving in temporarily to do the cooking, cleaning, and laundry, friends can be a lifeline when you are grieving and finding it difficult to function. Some friends pray, sing, hold vigil, or read comforting scripture aloud when you are overcome with grief and anxiety and need something to hold onto, need light in the darkness that feels unending. Some just sit, hold your hand and cry with you. If they are particularly intuitive, they recognize the times when what you need most is silence or solitude.

Sometimes, the people who support you are the family members of other patients when your loss was preceded by lengthy and/or multiple hospital stays. These are people who "get it," who know what you're going through and intuitively know what will be most helpful at any given moment in the ups and downs of end-of-life situations. Some of these people become friends who stay in touch long after the loss. Strong bonds are often created when people are thrown together during some of the worst times in their lives.

Eileen's Story

When word got out that Eileen's son was suffering from catastrophic liver failure and would likely die, one of the first people to call was her choir director, who had been a pastor of another denomination before he took the job at her church. When he heard the news, he came to the hospital as soon as he could, sensing that she needed someone there to lean on. From that moment on, this man shepherded Eileen and her husband through the agonizing three days in the hospital, helped make the necessary arrangements after their son's death, and officiated at the funeral. During that difficult time, he was her pastor in all but the most formal sense of the word. Her gratitude for his presence is immense.

Another kind gesture was made when her other son's in-laws graciously ceded their traditional time with him and their daughter on Mother's Day so he could be with his own parents for that difficult day. The in-laws and their entire family, including adult children and spouses, also attended the funeral despite not being of the same faith. This show of support was particularly touching for Eileen and her husband.

The Lord doesn't ask us to cheer up those who mourn or fix those who mourn or teach those who mourn. (God) asks us to mourn with those who mourn.[30]

—Hank Smith

What Not to Say

Sadly, not everyone has the emotional intelligence or intuition to know what is needed at any given moment in the days, weeks, and months after significant loss. People mean well but can say and do some of the most hurtful things. Following are some of those along with explanations and alternative, more helpful ways to respond

---

[30] Smith, https://twitter.com/hankrsmith/status/1305963351390871553?lang=en, September 15, 2020

when you are seeking to console a loved one who is grieving.

Everything happens for a reason. This does not make people feel better. It does not comfort anyone. It makes it clear that the speaker is uncomfortable with the grieving person's emotions and wants them to keep their feelings to themselves. Worse, it makes the one experiencing loss wonder what that reason was and whether God is purposefully punishing them. The reality is that we live in a random world. Bad things happen. Unavoidable accidents occur. People get sick. Pandemics don't play favorites, visiting illness and death on the good and the bad in equal measure. Criminals don't care who they hurt when they choose to cause harm to another human being. There is no hierarchy of who deserves bad things to happen and who does not. This is life. None of us get a pass on loss and pain and traumatic events.

God never gives you more than you can handle. Let me just emphatically deny that this so-called "promise" exists anywhere in the Bible! It *does* say that in all our trials and tribulations, which *will* come our way, God will be present with us through it all. To suggest that the death of a loved one is something we should be able to "handle" is just cruel.

You should be over this by now. An older couple who were clients of mine years ago had lost their adult daughter to bulimia. Their grief was agonizing to watch. But what really destroyed them is that a fellow parishioner in their church dared to approach them and suggest that they weren't strong enough Christians because they hadn't yet gotten over the loss of their daughter. This was wrong on so many levels! It's also another example of someone who is uncomfortable with other people's painful feelings and wants to say something that will make them go away.

I know just how you feel. No. Just no. You might have compassion for someone who is grieving and want to support them and validate their emotions, but none of us can ever know what someone else is feeling. Everyone is different. Everyone has had different life experiences that shape how they react to loss. And the relationship the grieving person had with the deceased makes a huge difference in how one responds to their death. Just because you also lost a friend or marital partner or sibling, et cetera, doesn't mean you know how someone in a similar situation is feeling. It's also not a good idea to tell someone in great detail about the loss you suffered that makes you *think* you know how the person you're addressing feels. It's not about you right now. It's about the person with the most immediate loss. If the grieving person *asks* you to talk about your grief because they know you have suffered a similar loss, *then* you can tell them.

God needed him/her more than you do. Again, this is not in the Bible! God doesn't *need* someone's loved one in heaven. Nobody living knows what heaven is like, but I can't imagine that God has work for us to do "up there." Our holy work is down here! This statement is especially painful when the deceased is a child, and someone says, "God needed another angel in heaven." This is not comforting and can be the cause of the hearer to lose their faith in God altogether.

At least he/she isn't suffering anymore. While this may be true, it's not comforting. Loss is loss, and even if you are grateful that your loved one's suffering is over, the grief is still there and must be acknowledged and muddled through.

He/she is with God now. When we have lost someone near and dear to us, our inner response to this statement might be to either tune the speaker out completely or to rebel, reject the message and think, "I don't care!! I just want my loved one *here,* with *me*!" Wherever their soul is residing seems inconsequential compared to the gaping hole their death has left in our lives, an ache that is sometimes too much to bear.

You're so strong. I'm pretty sure that most people who hear this statement feel anything but strong and wish they were stronger. The reality is that grieving people would give anything to not *need* to be strong. There is also an implication by the speaker that they value strength and don't want to have to deal with any weakness that might be displayed. The survivor isn't allowed to fully express everything that they're feeling.

You'll find someone else. Again, the speaker is trying to push the sufferer past their grief into a time when life is good again. Basically, it's the same as saying, "Get over it and get on with it." A corollary to this statement is, "He/she would want you to be happy." Ugh!

One final outrageous comment was made by a relative of Debby, whose young adult son was killed in a car accident, "Well, now you know how God felt when he lost his only son." Minimizing your loss by comparing it to what God might have felt at Jesus' death on the cross is just plain hurtful. If you have heard any of these statements in the aftermath of a loss, you are free to ignore them, refuse to respond to them, avoid the people who said them whenever possible, and otherwise dismiss the implications and give yourself permission to grieve in whatever way you need to. And find other friends.

When it seems that our sorrow
is too great to be borne, let us think of
the great family of the heavy-hearted
into which our grief has given us
entrance, and inevitably, we will feel
about us their arms, their sympathy,
their understanding.[31]
—Helen Keller

So, what <u>should</u> you do that would be helpful, kind, and compassionate if you are a friend to someone who has suffered a loss? First and foremost, remember that your presence is so much more important than your words. Be willing to just sit with someone, hold their hand, let them know that their tears are okay, that the tears are a measure of the person's love for the one who is gone. If you tear up yourself, let the tears fall. Just make sure that your emotions don't overpower theirs. If they seem like they want to talk, ask them to share their memories—funny moments, special moments, everyday rituals they shared, unique traits, et cetera. And just listen! It's okay to ask if they want to look through photographs with you that will bring up more memories. It's also okay if they aren't ready

---

[31] Quotesgram.com

for that yet. You can pray with them or read scriptures aloud, perhaps one of their favorite passages or some from the list of comforting scriptures at the back of this book.

As we've already discovered, grief has a physical as well as emotional toll. It's exhausting! And someone who is grieving is not going to have the energy or will to do many of the daily household tasks that need doing. Offer to help in specific ways. It's likely they are too overwhelmed to be able to name what actually needs to be done. So, offer to do the dishes, straighten up the living room, do laundry, dust, run errands, and so on. Offer to drive them to appointments, go with them as they make funeral arrangements, or just get groceries. Even the most mundane tasks may feel overwhelming in times of grief, so be alert to whatever might need to be done and ask if they'd like you to do it. In addition, those who are grieving often neglect self-care. Encourage them to be gentle with themselves. Suggest taking a walk together if the weather permits. Sunshine and fresh air do wonders for the soul, especially at such a time as this.

Above all, remember that while memory is short, grief is long. Many times, friends eventually go on with their own daily lives, forgetting that for the grieving one, life has changed forever, and their grief doesn't follow any predictable timetable. Stay in touch, whether by phone or with occasional cards or letters to let them know you are still thinking of them. In particular, touch base with them on the days that hold extra meaning—Mother's Day, Father's Day, birthdays, anniversaries, holidays, and so on.

After my mother died, I was chatting with a woman I didn't know well at a spiritual retreat. Somehow the conversation came around to my mother's death. She expressed her sympathy, and then our chat was cut short by the beginning of the event. Imagine my surprise when, several weeks later, I received a card in the mail from her just prior to Mother's Day. Her thoughtfulness touched me deeply. Having someone acknowledge that difficult day was especially meaningful for me.

Spiritual Practice

Sanctuary

Walking with one who grieves
is like entering a great cathedral
and sitting near
(but not too near)
the one who slumps in a pew,
weeping,
inconsolable.
And all you can do is weave prayers
around her,
breathe prayers that fly
in great spirals over his head,
like birds,
creating sanctuary,
offering peace.
All this is done quietly,
so quietly,
and when it is time to go,
tiptoeing,
trailing the scent of myrrh
behind you.

Take some time to sit with this poem. What emotions come up for you? While the images are metaphorical, consider how they might be translated into lived experience. Who are the people in your life that are as gentle and empathetic as the poem suggests? Who are those that are able to just sit quietly and hold your grief with you? Also, consider the places that might feel like sanctuary to you, where you might feel a sense of Divine Presence. You can journal your thoughts or write a prayer that expresses some of what you are feeling, particularly the gratitude you have for the friends who have been by your side during this time of grief.

Prayer

Divine Friend, I thank you for the gift of friends, companions on the way, for the ways in which I have been blessed by people who love me, who are willing to sit by my side through both good days and bad, who anticipate my needs, even when it is the need to be alone. Help me to forgive those who say hurtful things from a place of trying to be helpful. Remind me that it is also okay to distance myself from them. Help me remember that you are my greatest Friend, always present, always comforting, always aware of my deepest need. Amen.

Interlude

We are all holding hands,
clinging to each other,
stumbling over the hardscrabble
landscape
that is life.
Sometimes one of us
knows the terrain and leads.
Sometimes we are the followers,
trusting, hoping
there is an easier way,
but if not,
grateful at least
for the company.

(with a nod to Hafiz)

Chapter Ten

Integration, Transformation, and Hope

May those who sow in tears
Reap with shouts of joy.
Those who go out weeping,
Bearing the seed for sowing,
Shall come home with shouts of joy,
Carrying their sheaves.
—Psalm 126: 5-6 (NRSV)

Grief never ends, but it can be transformed. As I mentioned earlier, it becomes part of your story, but eventually it will no longer be the whole story. It will no longer dominate your every waking moment or impact your ability to function in daily life. You are able to integrate your loss into the wholeness of who you are. Grief shapes you, and the shaping can become a gift, making you more compassionate, more aware of the world's pain, more willing to become an instrument of healing for others.

On September 11, 1974, when comic and television personality Steven Colbert was ten years old, his father and two of his closest brothers by age died in an airplane crash as it was attempting to land in Charlotte, North Carolina.[32]

---

[32] En.wikipedia.org/wiki/Stephen Colbert, accessed 9/27/2023

They were en route to enroll the two boys at a school in Connecticut. Steven and his remaining family were devastated by this loss. Despite being the youngest, Steven took it upon himself to make his mother laugh, thus easing her grief. Later, his sense of humor became a significant factor in his television career, which has brought joy and laughter to the millions who watched his former show, *The Colbert Report*, or his current program, *The Late Show with Stephen Colbert.* When responding to an interviewer's question about the accident decades later, he made the comment, "Our sorrow is inseparable from our joy."

This statement echoes the writings of Kahlil Gibran in *The Prophet.* This small book of wisdom teachings addresses this seeming paradox. ". . . the selfsame well from which your laughter rises was oftentimes filled with your tears. And how else can it be? The deeper that sorrow carves into your being, the more joy you can contain."[33] The full text of this passage can be found in Chapter Two.

Grief and loss often become transformative. Life comes from death in many ways. In the cycle of the seasons, trees drop their seeds, acorns, and cones that become new trees fertilized in the mulch of fallen leaves. Rotting trees on the forest floor feed insects, which feed small animals, and so on in the cycle of life. Those same trees send up shoots of new growth as the forest propagates itself. When my husband and I visited Sequoia National Park many years ago, our guide shared a story about the germination of these mighty trees. The U.S. Forest Service had been taking great pains to protect the redwoods from wildfires. However, after some time had passed, they began

[33] Gibran, *The Prophet,* p.32

to notice that fewer and fewer seedlings were growing to replenish the forest. They were puzzled as to the reason for this lack of propagation. Then came a fire that was uncontrollable, and they were unable to keep it away from the sequoia groves. Of course, several of the majestic trees were lost in the fire, but eventually Forest Service rangers noticed that there were suddenly many new seedlings sprouting from the soil in areas where the fire had burned. Their conclusion was that heat from the forest fire had somehow aided in the germination process. Life from death, the eternal cycle, had taught them something they didn't know and ultimately saved the sequoia grove from dying off completely.

Jamie Raskin's Story

Jamie Raskin is a constitutional law professor and U.S. representative from the state of Maryland. He is widely respected and has served on many congressional committees, making a major impact in Washington, D.C. He and his wife raised a son and a daughter, Tommy and Tabitha. Tommy, a student at Harvard Law, had suffered from bouts of severe depression for several years. He was only at Harvard for six months when COVID hit, and he came home to continue his education online. On November 2, 2020, Jamie won his third term in the House and spent most of the evening watching election results with Tommy. Jamie would say later that his son looked particularly withdrawn that night. In mid-December, Tommy hosted an online Q & A session for Jamie's birthday but signed off after the introduction and first question. Later, on New Years Eve, Jamie and Tommy spent the evening together watching television and playing a game. They talked about their plans for the following day and went to bed. It was the last time Jamie would see his son alive. Sometime later that night, Tommy died by his own hand.

In his farewell note, Tommy said, "Please forgive me. My illness won today. Look after each other, the animals, and the global poor. All my love, Tommy." Six days later, a day after burying his son, Jamie took his daughter to Congress with him, the same day the Capitol building was attacked. The following week, Jamie was named lead manager of President Trump's second impeachment trial.

Despite his terrible grief, Congressman Raskin took on that task, viewing it as a lifeline that could pull him out of the sorrow in which he was drowning. He had doubted that he would ever be able to do anything worthwhile or meaningful again after losing his son. Nonetheless, he stepped up to take on that role just twelve days after Tommy's death. He continues to serve in Congress and to fight for social justice for the poor and integrity in government, living up to the challenge his son expressed in his final words. Now three years later, Jamie says, "Tommy lives on in each of us. What matters is the love of others. Your love can become the engine of a quest for justice."[34]

Candy Lightner was another bereaved parent who used her anger and pain at losing her daughter to fight for stronger drunk driving laws. Carime was only thirteen when a man with a history of drunk driving mowed her down with his car and left the scene. This catapulted Candy

---

[34] "Love and the Constitution" documentary, MSNBC, 2022.

into a quest to reduce the numbers of children harmed or killed by drunk drivers. As a result of her work through Mothers Against Drunk Drivers (MADD), the organization she founded, the national drinking age was raised to 21, and the penalties for drunk driving were increased in most states in the United States as well as Canada.[35]

When people like Jamie Raskin and Candy Lightner use their grief as fuel for redemptive action, they transform their pain into avenues that make a difference in the world and make meaning of their loss. Now, most of us don't have the wherewithal to get elected to a position in government or to create a national organization, but there are many ways that we can redeem the loss of a loved one by finding meaningful ways to make a difference in the world. We can contribute to the charities they supported or volunteer for a non-profit that in some way works to help eradicate disease, make the world safer, or change harmful laws. These kinds of activities keep the memory of your loved one alive and continue their legacy for generations to come.

Certainly, these types of activities are one way to maintain an ongoing bond with your lost loved one. Living your life in a way that you know would make them proud is affirming of the love you shared, the admiration you feel about what they accomplished in life, and a way of helping them live on long after they are gone. There will be times, when you have achieved a goal which your loved one supported, that you will feel them near, applauding your accomplishments from the beyond. When my first book was published three years after my father had passed and

[35] "Mothers Against Drunk Driving," Wikipedia, accessed 2023.

eight years after my mother, I felt their presence very strongly. I knew how extremely proud they would have been. It was a bittersweet moment. I missed them fiercely, but I also knew that they were still with me, cheering me on.

The world breaks everyone and afterward many are strong at the broken places.[36]
—Ernest Hemingway

I was visiting my daughter in another state years ago, and we went out to breakfast one morning. As I was washing my hands in the restroom, I couldn't help but notice that the walls were tiled with broken, multi-colored pottery. I asked my daughter if she knew the story behind this unique wall décor. She told me the restaurant had ordered some custom coffee mugs to be made, but when they were shipped, some of the boxes had been damaged in transit, and a large number of the mugs had been broken. Rather than throw away the broken shards, the manager decided to use the pieces to create the mosaic that now decorated their bathroom walls. I had a visceral reaction to this, realizing what a powerful message it was, that even that which is broken can be turned into something beautiful.

In the Japanese art of kintsugi, broken pottery is sometimes repaired with gold. The resulting effect is beautiful. The formerly broken places shine brightly and

---

[36] Hemingway, *A Farewell to Arms,* cited in goodreads.com/quotes/6592630, as of 9/22/2023

give the object more beauty than it had in its original form. It also strengthens the object, allowing it to be whole, to serve its purpose for many more years to come. I believe this is an apt metaphor for grief. We are broken by the losses we experience. We are drowning in our sorrow and sometimes feel as if we can't go on, that the future looks bleak and devoid of joy. And yet, so often in my therapy practice, I saw patients who found a path into a new way of living, found people and/or causes that helped them feel alive again, useful again, able to reenter the world around them and even experience contentment. They were able to find meaning and purpose despite their losses. This is the hidden treasure, the small yet tenacious ember, that lies deep beneath the ashes of loss, that we can heal our grief, weave it tenderly into the story of who we are, become more compassionate and loving, stronger than we could ever imagine, and ultimately share this message with those we companion on their own journeys of grief. It is this treasure that reminds us that even in death, love abides.

Spiritual Practice

Sequoia Grove

Ancient sentinels stand,
bulwarks against the ravages
of wind, fire, and time.
Their bark bears mute testimony
to nature's power to heal.
Deep scars tell tales
of tragic wounds,
and still they grow, survive,

lend grace and beauty
to the eternal forest.
Listen to their story.
Perhaps it speaks
to your struggles
and to mine.

Forest floor,
sweetly perfumed with the tang
of decayed needles,
is littered with cones
carrying the seeds of life.
Fire is their baptism,
their birth, their release
into creative energy.
Then buried and blanketed
by the mulch of gentle death,
they grow in secret,
until green springs forth
and another cycle of
life and death begins.
Can this not enflame
your hope
and mine?

How does this poem speak to you about the cycle of life and death and the transformative power of grief? Consider writing your own poem about the loss you have experienced and how it has changed you, made you more compassionate, more tender-hearted. How does this theme of life and death in an eternal cycle fit with your own spiritual beliefs?

Prayer

Loving and transforming God, be with us in our sorrow. Walk beside us as we travel through this dark valley. And when the grieving time has passed, continue to guide us, leading us to new and healing pathways. Help us find meaning in our loss. Help us to believe that we can re-enter the land of the living, choose life in all its abundance and live in ways that honor our loved ones and help to continue their legacy in the world. Amen.

Benediction

Surrender

It is not enough to look into the abyss,
to peer into the darkness. Rather,
one must surrender oneself to it—
fall—
land in the belly of the whale,
learn the lessons of darkness.
Receive the wisdom of unknowing.
Receive the love that awaits you there
when you thought you had lost everything.
Discover that the bottom of the pit
is the only path to redemption,
transformation.
And then climb.

Acknowledgements

This book would never have happened were it not for a caring and insightful comment about my own grief in the aftermath of COVID (see Introduction) from my dear friend, Juli Reinholz. She is sadly no longer with us, but she will be in my heart forever. Her husband David has given me thoughtful and wise comments as I have shared this work with him. I also want to thank the usual suspects—my grown children and my husband, who are my biggest supporters and tolerate my times of withdrawal as I hunker down at my computer for hours on end. I was blessed to receive invaluable feedback from Daniel Wolpert, author of *Creating A Life with God*. Last but most assuredly not least, I will be forever grateful to all those who shared their grief stories with me. Your experiences inspired and humbled me, and you are the essence of this book.

Recommended Reading

Bessey, Sarah (ed.), *A Rhythm of Prayer,* Convergent Books, 2020

Gibran, Kahlil, *The Prophet,* 1923

O'Rourke, Michelle, *Befriending Death: Henri Nouwen and a Spirituality of Dying,* Orbis Books, 2009.

Richardson, Jan, *Circle of Grace,* Wanton Gospeller Press, 2015

Richardson, Jan, *The Cure for Sorrow,* Wanton Gospeller Press, 2016

Riley, Cole Arthur, *This Here Flesh,* Convergent Books, 2022

Smith, Jenny, *Still Here: a poetry memoir of grief & love,* Amazon Kindle, 2023

Taylor, Barbara Brown, *God in Pain: Teaching Sermons on Suffering,* Abingdon Press, 2010

Warren, Tish Harrison, *Prayer in the Night*, InterVarsity Press, 2021

Weller, Francis, *The Wild Edge of Sorrow,* North Atlantic Books, 2015

Psalms of Lament

Psalm 5
Psalm 6
Psalm 10,
Psalm 12
Psalm 13
Psalm 14
Psalm 22 (which is interestingly followed by Psalm 23)
Psalm 42
Psalm 43
Psalm 60
Psalm 61
Psalm 77
Psalm 88
Psalm 130
Psalm 137
Lamentations 2: 18-19, 21-22

Biblical Comfort

Psalm 23
Psalm 30
Psalm 40:1-5
Psalm 46
Psalm 121
Psalm 126
Isaiah 49:13-15
Isaiah 61:1-3
Jeremiah 31:9-13
Lamentations 3:22-26, 31-33
Matthew 5:4

References

Berry, Wendell, *Jayber Crow: A Novel,* Counterpoint, 2001

Bessey, Sarah (ed.), *A Rhythm of Prayer,* Convergent Books, 2020

"Stephen Colbert," Wikipedia, accessed 9/27/2023

Eslinger, Elise, ed., *Upper Room Worshipbook,* Upper Room Books, 2006

Gibran, Kahlil, *The Prophet,* 1923

"The Promise of a New Day," Hazeldon Meditation Series, July 27th reading, 1983

Hemingway, Ernest, *A Farewell to Arms,* Scribner, 1929, quote as cited in *goodreads.com.*

Job, Rueben & Shawchuck, Norman, eds., *A Guide to Prayer for All God's People,* Upper Room Books, 1990

"Love and the Constitution" television documentary, MSNBC, 2022

"Mothers Against Drunk Driving," Wikipedia, accessed 2023

O'Rourke, Michelle, *Befriending Death: Henri Nouwen and a Spirituality of Dying,* Orbis Books, 2009

Peterson, Eugene, *Tell It Slant: A Conversation on the Language of Jesus,* Eerdmans, 2012

Richardson, Jan, *Circle of Grace,* Wanton Gospeller Press, 2015

Richardson, Jan, *The Cure for Sorrow,* Wanton Gospeller Press, 2016

Riley, Cole Arthur, *This Here Flesh,* Convergent Books, 2022

Rohr, Richard, *Communal Lament,* Center for Action and Contemplation, July 27, 2021

Smith, Hank, https://twitter.com/hankrsmith, September 15, 2020

Sweet Honey in the Rock, *Breaths* (record album), Flying Fish Records, 1988

Taylor, Barbara Brown, *God in Pain: Teaching Sermons on Suffering,* Abingdon Press, 2010

United Methodist Hymnal, United Methodist Publishing House, 1989

Warren, Tish Harrison, *Prayer in the Night*, InterVarsity Press, 2021

Weller, Francis, *The Wild Edge of Sorrow,* North Atlantic Books, 2015

Made in the USA
Middletown, DE
03 September 2024

60342514R00099